PROFITS IN VOLUME

EQUIVOLUME CHARTING

RICHARD W. ARMS JR.

INVESTORS INTELLIGENCE

Copyright ©1971 by Richard W. Arms
Published by Marketplace Books.

ISBN 1-883272-25-4

Printed in the United States of America.

1234567890 K 54321098

CONTENTS

PREFACE
TO THE SECOND EDITION

It has been over a quarter of a century since this book first appeared in print. Yet, as I look through it again, and add an introduction to it, I find it amazingly current, in every way except the illustrations. With today's computer graphics and with technical analysis available through a number of excellent programs, everyone is able to have professional looking charts at his fingertips. By those standards the charts look somewhat primitive. But they illustrate the ideas well, and the hand drawn charts have a simplicity I had almost forgotten. Moreover, the ideas have not changed. Time has not forced revision, but only amplification. The principles of Equivolume remain today as they were first put forth in this book.

In 1971, I was working as a retail stockbroker for a large New York Stock Exchange member firm. By then I had already developed my Arms Index, although, at that time it was still known as The Short Term Trading Index. I think, even then, I had become aware that volume played a far larger part in technical analysis than most people realized. It was, of course, volume, which made the Arms Index a unique tool. Following the comparison of advances to declines was a mainstay of technical analysis, but no one had inserted volume into the calculation. This index, which compared advances and declines to advancing and declining volume, presented a different perspective. (The last two chapters of this book explain the index in detail.)

At that time I was also becoming disillusioned with the Wall Street research with which I was expected to advise my clients. It had become increasingly apparent to me that research, especially research designed for the use of the retail brokers, was meant to help in the generation of commissions for the company and for the broker, but not necessarily in the generation of profits for clients. I had lost confidence in the advice I was getting from headquarters. And if I did not have confidence I certainly could not create confidence in my clients. I felt I needed to develop my own ideas, if I was to help my clients make money.

I knew a bit about technical analysis, of course, I had worked with point and figure charts as well as bar charts, and I subscribed to a chart service which provided me with weekly updated bar charts. I decided to pay what was then to me a quite high price, $500, to study the methods of Richard Wyckoff, through the *Wyckoff School of Technical Analysis*. It was a wonderful course, in which each student periodically received stock charts and audiotapes analyzing them. In addition, the original ideas of Richard Wyckoff were presented in a pair of books, each with its own padlock. It was like being allowed to share in a deep secret. To me, it was the opening of a door to a better approach to the market. I remember being particularly impressed with the fact that they placed heavy emphasis on volume.

One afternoon, while driving home from the office, I was mulling over some of the ideas from the course, and remembered a particular observation Bob Evans, the narrator of the tapes, had made. He said something along these lines: "If a stock goes down through an old area of support with increasing volume and a widening of the spread it cannot be a selling climax; it must be a sign of weakness." It suddenly occurred to me that the key the volume could be depicted more emphatically. It was not just the price move that was important nor was it just the volume, it was the combination of the two. Yet, on a chart, we did not combine these two factors, we plotted them separately. If the two pieces of information were to be combined into a single entry it would be a far better way of recognizing significant action. By the time I reached home the entire concept of Equivolume had taken shape in my mind. I would move the volume off the bottom border of the chart, where it had been relegated as an afterthought, and combine it with the price. In that way each posting would be a box instead of a line, with the width of the box being the volume.

It seemed like a great idea, but it seemed extremely unlikely it could be a new idea. When I invented the Arms Index I had the advantage that the upside and downside volume data had not been compiled until just recently. I was just the first person to get around to putting the numbers together. But my idea for another way of drawing charts was a different situation. The data had always been available. A concept as ridiculously simple as to combine the volume and the price into a single posting could not have slipped by the thousands of people who had studied markets over the years. After all, point and figure was a much more complex methodology and it had been used for many years. I did some quiet checking, and could not find any such method being used. Perhaps, I thought, it had been tried and abandoned as useless. Well, it made too much sense for me to abandon it until I too had tried it, so I started to put the concept to use.

Once I had worked out the mechanics, so that the boxes would be properly scaled, I started to draw a number of charts, gleaning data from back issues of *The Wall Street Journal*. It seemed to work! I felt as though I was better able to feel the buying and selling pressures in a stock using this new graphic method. Perhaps it was valid, and perhaps it was new! I wondered if I should just keep it to myself and use it, or if I should reveal it to others I decided to try to write a book about these new charts but they needed a name. Since the basic change I had made in the method of chart construction was the placing of volume instead of time on the horizontal axis, it made it possible to measure equal amounts of volume with a ruler. Therefore, why not call it equal volume charting, or perhaps combine the words to Equivolume.

It was quite a number of years after this book had been out before I received a phone call from the well-known technician, John Bollinger. He was the technical analyst with the *Financial News Network* at that time. He pointed out to me that my idea was not new. In fact, he said, he had a publication in which the chartist had placed volume on the "X" axis long before I ever did. (Later, in fact, I had the opportunity to see some of those beautifully drawn charts). The man's name was Edwin S. Quinn, and he had done his work in the late 1940's. I had not invented the method, I had reinvented it! What I find surprising is that the method had not taken hold at the time.

Since this book was first published I have found it necessary to write two other books which dealt, at least in part, with Equivolume Yet, all I was doing was elaborating on the original work It was perhaps implicit in the original work that the Equivolume method produced wave patterns, but I felt it necessary to delve deeper into that concept. I also devised a method of reducing the box shapes and sizes into a numerical equivalent, which I called Ease of Movement. It was not, however, a change in the method, but a variation. I also found a way to construct moving average lines that were adjusted for volume. They were essentially Equivolume moving average lines. These were all variations and extensions of the work that appears in this book.

This book tells you how to draw Equivolume charts by hand, which was what I did for many years. Today there are a number of commercially available technical analysis programs that make Equivolume very easy. But this makes it almost too easy. I suggest that you keep charts by hand for a while, in order to appreciate the validity of the method. Only by drawing those little boxes yourself will you start to understand the importance of the factors which contribute to their size and shape. You will begin to realize that price and volume are partners, and that price range is an important consideration. After you become familiar with the hand drawn charts you will then want to get a good computer program. Only in that way will you be able to follow a large number of stocks. You will be able to change instantly from a daily chart to a weekly or monthly chart. You will be able to insert search formulas to find the most interesting situations. You will soon learn to look briefly at any chart, and be able to decide whether it needs further analysis. I often flip through many hundreds of charts on my computer, in the space of less than an hour, watching for the obvious buys and sells. As a money manager I go first to the individual stock charts. They often point me to the industries in which I wish to concentrate my holdings. I use overall market studies to help me in deciding how much money should be committed to stocks.

Since this book was first published technology has changed, but the principles of Equivolume remain the same. Every method in this book is just as usable today, on a computer drawn chart, as it was when first suggested. The great advantage of the technology is the ability to look at a great deal more information more easily It frees the analyst to be a chart-watcher rather than a chart-constructor. I hope this book and these methods will help every reader make more profitable market decisions.

Richard W. Arms, Jr.

Albuquerque, New Mexico
March 1998

INTRODUCTION

Two schools of thought exist regarding the behavior of the stock market. The first consists of those who believe that the stock market is an orderly meeting place of buyers and sellers, who exchange stocks when they feel that the values which the stocks represent have changed. They believe that the price of a stock is the logical outgrowth of that company's earning capacity, future prospects, backlog of orders, dividend payments and hundreds of other similar factors. They feel that by knowing and carefully analyzing these factors they can recognize issues which should be selling at higher or lower prices than the current market price. In short, they believe that the price of a stock is logical. If the market does not do what they expect of it, they assume that they analyzed the stock incorrectly, or missed some very important piece of information.

The second group visualizes stock prices as an outgrowth of human emotions, devoid of all logic. They believe that the main factors affecting stock prices are not earnings and dividends, but a delicate balance between the two emotions: fear and greed. To this group the price of a stock is determined by what people are willing to pay for it, and has no connection with the earning capacity of the company. These people try to recognize stocks which are in demand and capitalize on that demand, riding with the move, and letting the emotionalism of the market make money for them.

These two groups could be compared to other groups in a different field: religious believers and atheists. Where the stock market "believer" must accept on faith, the atheist throws out all belief, and becomes a complete pragmatist.

Regardless of his religious persuasion, we would ask the reader of this book to become a stock market agnostic. If he wishes to make money in the stock market we believe that he should accept the fundamental factors that govern the fates of corporations, but realize that these factors are beyond his analysis and interpretation. He must know that emotions play a large part in stock prices, but realize that trying to capitalize on these emotions without carefully analyzing and interpreting them can lead to financial disaster.

Perhaps the best way to follow this idea is to visualize a very large computer, into which all of the factors affecting a stock are carefully fed. These factors are more than just the company's latest financial statement, or a list of its board of directors. It includes the recent price action of the stock, and of the market in general. It can involve a casual remark the president of the company made over a Saturday evening bridge game; it includes how the manager of a large mutual fund felt this morning, and his subsequent attitude toward the acquisition of the stock. It involves every factor which could conceivably play any part in any investor's or group of investors' decisions in buying or selling this stock. After feeding all of the information into the computer, we push the "compute" button, and it prints out the price at which the stock should be trading.

This computer does in fact exist, and is already programmed. It is called "The Investing Public" and its output is available in every brokerage office, and is recapped in most newspapers. The millions of modules which make up the computer are human brains, sifting through all the fundamental and technical factors, buying stocks and selling stocks for all of their millions of individual reasons, and coming out with only two significant pieces of information: the price and volume of the stock.

In this book we will be concerned with the interpretation of this computer output. We realize that there are factors upon which people base their decisions, and that emotions are only a part of the total picture, but being stock market agnostics, we will strive to analyze the results of these factors, and thereby project probable price moves in the future.

CHAPTER I

METHODS OF TECHNICAL ANALYSIS

When the exchange closes and stocks cease trading for the day there are only two pieces of information left for the technical analyst to deal with: the prices of stocks and the volume on which those prices were established. All of the emotions and all of the facts relating to each company have boiled down to these two bits of information. It is the job of the analyst to try to properly correlate this information, and reach correct decisions as to future price action.

It is obvious then, that in this book all we can present is a new method of correlating this information in an attempt to reach more reliable conclusions. We still have only price and volume to work with, but we will try to emphasize different relationships that are brought out by these two factors. Previously, volume has always been regarded by technicians as a minor piece of information, to be put along the lower margin of the chart, and only referred to in passing, with the emphasis almost entirely upon the price. Very little has been done in an attempt to relate price action to volume. In addition, there has always been a tendency to pay the most attention to price changes, rather than ranges. We will show the price range to be the most important consideration next to volume.

Before looking closely at this new method of stock analysis, we must review the other major charting methods, and find their strengths and weaknesses. This groundwork is necessary in order to understand Equivolume Charting.

At the present time, there are only two widely accepted methods of depicting stock market behavior. These are vertical line charts and point and figure charts. As we shall see, both have their strengths and their weaknesses.

Vertical Line Charts. This method of charting places prices on the vertical axis, and time on the horizontal axis. Each day's trading range is depicted by a vertical line, the top of the line being the highest point at which the stock traded during that day, and the bottom being the lowest point at which the stock traded. There is attached to this line a small horizontal line which shows the price at which the stock closed for the day. Some chartists and chart publication services stop here, but most include volume figures across the bottom of the chart. The higher the vertical volume line the more volume during that trading session. (See Figure 1.)

There are many variations upon this, such as different time periods, so that each vertical line represents a week, a month or a year, but in any case, the horizontal scale remains constant. Many chartists prefer to use a logarithmic vertical scale, rather than an arithmetic one, so that percentage changes always appear in the same way. In addition, work has been done depicting the volume in two manners, such as two different colors, or solid lines and dashed lines to indicate upside volume and downside volume.

Vertical line charts are the oldest and most widely used method of charting, and are certainly an easily understood and worthwhile method of depicting stock

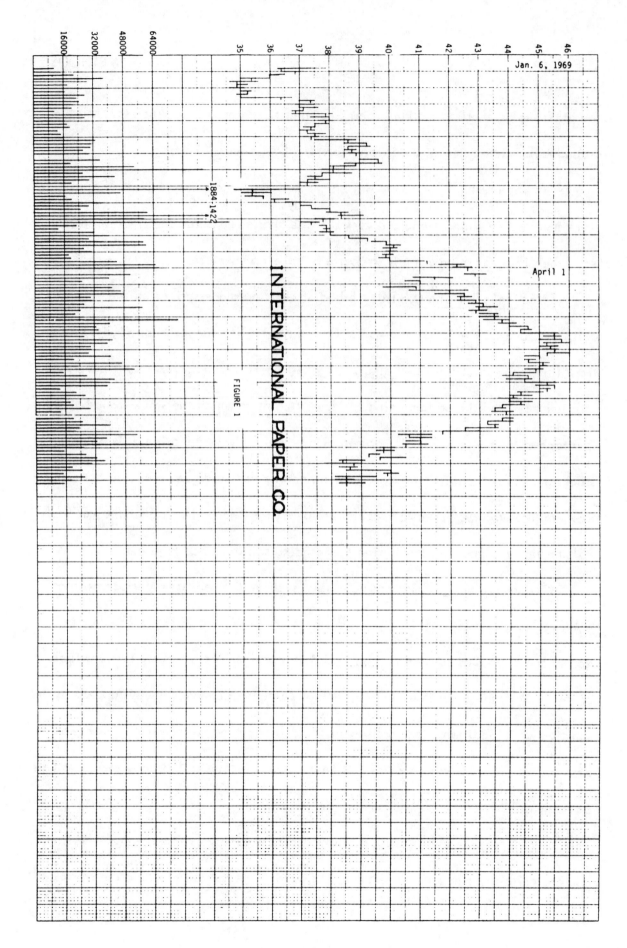

FIGURE 1

INTERNATIONAL PAPER CO.

market activity. Their attributes far overshadow their drawbacks.

Advantages and Disadvantages. The biggest single advantage of vertical line charts is that they are easily read and understood by anyone, after only a few seconds of explanation. They present a good visual impression of the present price of the stock as compared to where it has recently been. In addition, it is easy to see how volatile the stock is. The fact that time is a constant along the horizontal axis is important, in that the student can very easily relate price moves to time periods. Vertical line charts depict daily trading ranges well, also.

The volume figures which appear at the bottom of most charts are extremely important. It is possible on a vertical line chart to relate volume to the price moves on a given date. We feel, in fact, that the volume figures are so important that a chart which omits volume is close to being useless as a means of reaching logical market decisions.

Many of the factors which make vertical line charts good also contain the drawbacks of the system. The most important single drawback is the difficulty in correctly correlating volume and price. The analyst finds himself constantly going from the prices to volume figures, and trying to ascertain what goes with what. In addition, he is hard pressed to compare volumes in different parts of the chart. This is especially true if the analyst puts as much emphasis upon the trading range as we do. It is next to impossible to equate volume with trading range correctly on a vertical line chart.

The fact that the horizontal axis represents time is also a slight drawback. It makes it necessary to give every day equal weight. Each trading session is assigned

one vertical line, whether one thousand or one hundred thousand shares traded on
that day. This idea will be discussed further in the next chapter.

Point and Figure Charts. Although the system was known earlier, the point
and figure chart was not widely used or understood prior to the work of Richard
Wyckoff in the early 1930s. In this method of charting it is assumed that time is of
little importance, and that the primary factor is price movement. The idea is that
more price movement indicates more stock moving between the professionals and the
amateurs. At the bottom of the market the amateurs are selling and the professionals
are accumulating, and exactly the opposite is occurring at the top of a market.

In order to depict this, price remains on the vertical axis but the horizontal
axis represents price activity. Every time the stock being charted changes direction
the chartist moves one column to the right, and posts the price by placing an x in
the box representing the price. As long as the stock continues to move in the same
direction he will place more x's up or down the same column. Only when the stock
again changes its direction will he move to a new column. (See Figure 2.)

There are many variations upon this. The sensitivity can be varied by changing the amount of price reversal that is necessary in order to move to the next column.
For example, a three-point reversal chart requires that the stock move three points
or more in the opposite direction before it is considered a reversal, and before a new
column is begun. In addition, the vertical scale is often varied so that each square
represents two points or more. The reader who is unfamiliar with point and figure
charting may find this brief explanation difficult to understand. However, if he

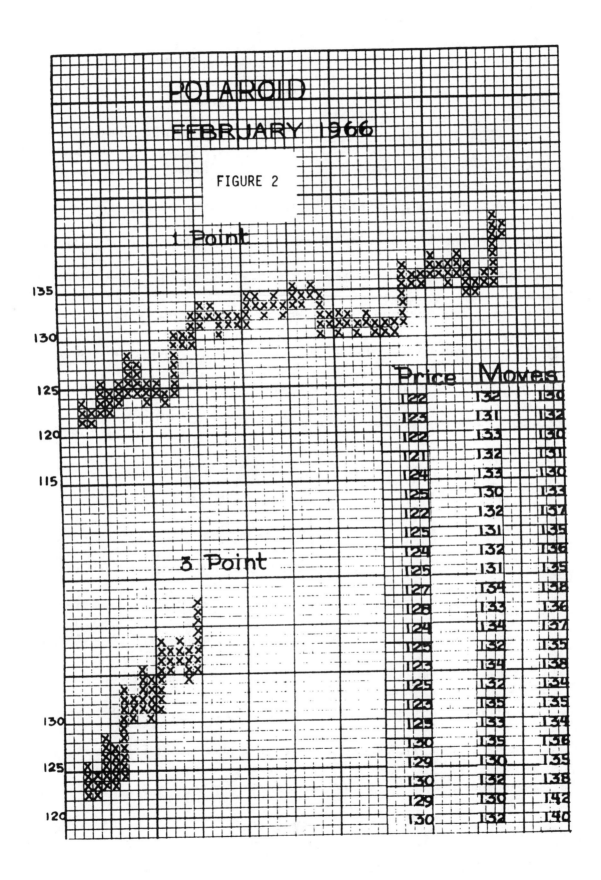

understands the ideas and reasoning behind point and figure charting that is all that will be necessary within the scope of this book.

Advantages and Disadvantages. Richard Wyckoff felt that the more a stock moved back and forth while within a trading range, the further the stock would move up or down once it broke out of its trading range. He considered point and figure to be primarily a tool for predicting the probable extent of market moves. For this it serves remarkably well. The width of a base is a very reliable indicator as to the extent of the ensuing move. Most of the drawbacks to point and figure are due to later technicians who have tried to use point and figure as a method of predicting market action rather than just price objectives. Through the use of trendlines and various patterns they have attempted to do all of their analysis from point and figure charts alone.

On point and figure charts time is extremely hard to ascertain, and volume is non-existent. There is no way of knowing how much stock changed hands at a given price, and it is usually very difficult to tell when the trading which established the price occurred. If a stock is moving fast, it may form a number of reversals, and therefore a number of columns in a single trading day. At another time it may not post any x's at all for days on end as it continues to trade in a narrow range.

In the next chapter we will introduce a method of charting which contains the advantages of point and figure and vertical line charts and eliminates most of the disadvantages of both. It is called "Equivolume Charting."

CHAPTER II

EQUIVOLUME CHARTING - THE REASONING BEHIND IT

The basic difference between Equivolume charting and all other charting

methods is the horizontal axis. As we have seen in the previous chapter, both verti-

cal line charts and point and figure charts place prices on the vertical axis. On the

horizontal axis point and figure charts use price reversals, while vertical line charts

use time. In Equivolume charting the horizontal axis represents volume: therefore

the name of the system. Equal distances on the horizontal axis reflect an equal a-

mount of stock changing hands.

Figure 3 shows a typical Equivolume chart. Each day of trading is represent-

ed by a rectangle, rather than a single line as in vertical line charts. The vertical

dimension of the rectangle represents the trading range, while the horizontal dimen-

sion reflects the volume in the stock during that trading day. As can be seen, there

is no question of assigning the correct volume to the correct trading day. The two

parts of the vertical line charts, the price and the volume, have been combined into

one understandable entry.

The Importance of Trading Range. Equivolume charting makes a very radical

departure from all other systems in that it stresses the trading range of a stock. We

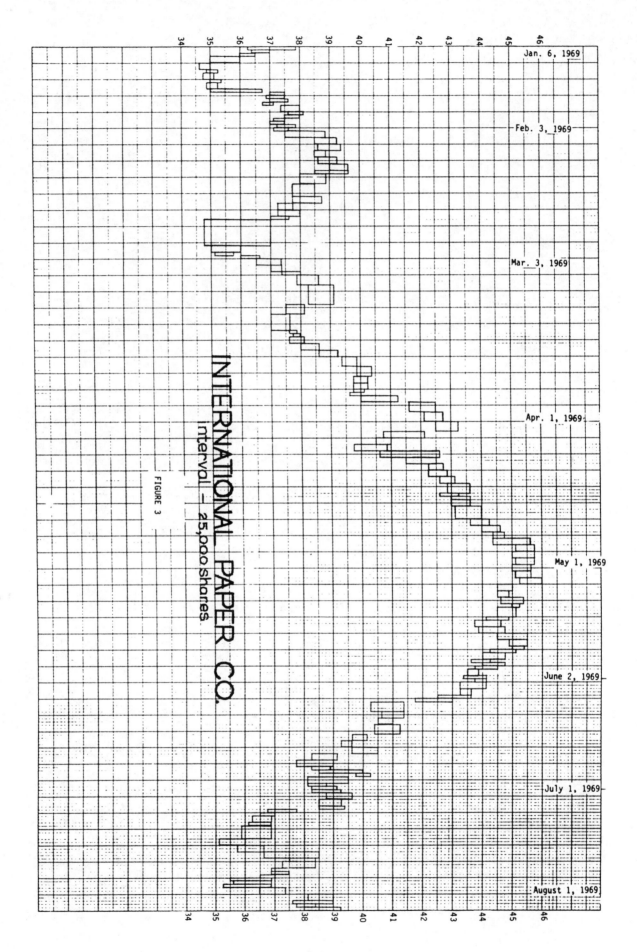

INTERNATIONAL PAPER CO.

Interval — 25,000 shares

FIGURE 3

believe that the trading range and the volume are the two primary factors involved in technical security analysis. They give an accurate appraisal of the supply and demand factors which are influencing a stock.

Although the trading range is represented on vertical line charts, it is not as obvious as it is on Equivolume charts. There is a tendency when working with vertical line charts to ignore the range, and concentrate on the extent of price moves, day to day. The result is that an extremely important factor is hardly being used in analyzing the stock.

The market is not a steady flow of trading. Out of every twenty-four hours in a weekday, only five and one-half are trading hours. The remainder of the day the market is closed. Only during market hours are stocks able to balance supply and demand, and come up with a price which the public is willing to pay for the stocks. The trading range represents the variety of different prices at which the public was willing to exchange the shares in a company during a single session. By studying the trading range we can see how easy or difficult it is for a stock to move.

If the range of a stock during a trading session is very small, that stock is evidently meeting with opposition to any move. If it tries to move up, there is evidently stock waiting to be sold, and if it tries to move down, there are buyers present. A wide trading range, on the other hand, reflects fairly easy movement. Either the buyers or the sellers are backing away, and the price is having to move for trades to be consummated.

On the other hand, studying price changes is of little value. If a stock closes on its high of the day today, after closing on its low yesterday, the net price change may be quite large. It is possible, however, that on both days the stock traded in the same trading range, and the net change is meaningless.

Market Equilibrium. Generally we have very little idea why a stock moves up or down an eighth between trades. There are certainly no fundamental factors which make a stock worth more ten minutes from now than it is right now. The only way to realistically look at these minor moves is to attribute them to a myriad of factors which are probably known only to the individuals making the trades. A seller may have to pay for a new car, or he may be switching to another stock which he considers more attractive. The buyer may have some worthwhile information about the company, but he may also be acting on a "tip" from his barber. The individual reasons mean nothing to us, but the overall effect is worth our consideration.

The basic premise upon which the market operates is that the highest bid and the lowest offer have priority on the floor of the exchange. When a trade takes place these two are the same. The buyer has to be willing to meet the seller's price, or vice versa, or no trade takes place. When the buyer and seller agree on a price an equilibrium has been reached, and at that instant the value of that stock has been established. Between trades the value of the stock has been closely bracketed by the bid and asked prices, but an equilibrium does not exist. Essentially there is a small disagreement between the buyers and the sellers as to the value of the stock. Each time a trade is consummated an equilibrium is established, but a buyer and a seller have been eliminated from the marketplace, and new factors come into play which will decide the price at which buyer and seller again agree upon a price.

The above discussion may appear to the reader to be looking too closely at the very minor moves, but it is these moves, when put together, that make up the trading day, and give us the information upon which we must base our investment decisions. As each individual transaction takes place it reveals to the analyst the status of supply and demand in the marketplace. As trading progresses, if the sellers have more stock to sell, than the buyers want to absorb, prices will have to move downward. In addition, if holders of the stock are worried about the company, or the economy, they may be more anxious to sell than the buyers are to buy. In this case also the stock will move down. In Equivolume charting our primary concern will be with analysis of the supply-demand balance.

Volume and Its Importance. No single factor involved in stock market analysis is more important or misunderstood than volume. Its analysis can be the basis for successful trading if it is used correctly, yet very few analysts use it correctly. For example, there is a tendency for most market commentators, and especially brokers, to believe that heavy upside trading in a stock is a good sign. A quick look at a few charts should make it fairly obvious that the heaviest trading in a stock almost invariably occurs right at the top. Similarly, heavy downside volume is always spoken of as a bad sign. Look at a few stocks, though, and you will see that heavy trading is often a sign that a decline is ending.

In this book we will be constantly studying volume, and attempting to determine investor sentiment by it. The number of shares that change hands are our best indication of how anxious the buyers are to buy and the sellers are to sell. In addition, heavy volume in a stock is very often reflecting large block transactions. This serves as an indication of the activity of institutions in the stock we are studying.

The Volume-Range Relationship. We have now looked at the importance of range and volume. It is in the combination of these two factors that Equivolume serves its purpose. Looking at the range in which a stock trades gives us a fairly good idea how tight the trading is. That is, a narrow trading range indicates that the supply and demand factors are close to a balance, and neither buyers nor sellers are able to get the upper hand. A wide trading range indicates a large discrepancy between the buyers and the sellers. The price moves rapidly, because a steady balance of supply and demand does not exist. Similarly, studying volume alone gives us a good idea as to how anxious the traders are as they move a stock upward or downward.

When these two factors are combined, we are observing the exact force of the buying and selling pressures. It is obviously more significant when a stock moves one-half point on 1000 shares than it would be if it moves one-eighth of a point on the same 1000 shares. By combining volume and spread we are able to see the ease or difficulty with which that stock is moving. As is readily seen, this puts volume figures in a different light. Rather than trying to say that volume is good or bad in an uptrend or a downtrend, we are seeing how easy or hard it is for the stock to move at this time. We immediately become conscious of pressures on the stock which would have been almost unnoticeable in a vertical line chart. A narrow spread with fairly heavy volume shows up as a short wide day. Evidently the stock is meeting some resistance to its current up or down move. Although volume is heavy, the stock is unable to progress. By studying this day in context, as we will in later chapters, we can tell whether it is overhead supply that is restricting the stock or downside demand that is holding it up.

Similarly, a day in which the stock moves through a fairly wide trading range on light volume can provide us with worthwhile information. A day of this sort would provide a tall, narrow rectangle on the Equivolume chart, and would indicate that the stock is finding movement to be very easy. It takes few shares to move it up or down. Evidently the stock is not being hindered by either a heavy supply or a large demand.

The important thing about Equivolume charting is that every day is telling a story. No trading session becomes unimportant, because each entry is telling us how easy that stock is finding it to move. This will allow us to be more objective on our investments and reduce the emotional decisions which so often end up costing us money.

How About the Closing Price? One feature on vertical line charts which is omitted on Equivolume charts is the closing price. The omission is intentional; they would be very easy to include. In fact we included it in some of the original work with this method, but then decided to omit it. The reason is simple; people pay too much attention to closing prices. Many people read only the closing prices of their stocks in the newspaper, and base their decisions on this figure. They are influenced by the net change from the previous day's closing price, and interpret the stock's action by these figures.

The closing price is only one trade out of the entire day of trading, and it may be at the top or the bottom of the trading range. It may reflect a large block, but is more likely to reflect a few hundred shares only. We can see no magic reason for assigning this price a position of prominence. It is just another trade, and is reflected in our trading rectangle for the day represented. To enter is again is to give it extra weight which can throw off our judgment. The closing price plays no special part in our supply-demand equation.

As we have seen, Equivolume charting can provide all of the information found on a vertical line chart, and present it in a more easily analyzed manner. Since each day is a separate entry there is no problem in recognizing time intervals, although time is not constant as it is on the horizontal axis of a vertical line chart. A later chapter which deals with price objectives will point out how this method also provides the advantages of a point and figure chart, without its drawbacks, and by going directly to the volume rather than the roundabout method of reaching price objectives by looking at the number of price reversals.

CHAPTER III

EQUIVOLUME CHART CONSTRUCTION

Equivolume charting calls for no equipment nor techniques which are not already known to anyone who has ever charted a stock using vertical line charts. The only real difference is the use of volume on the horizontal axis.

Chart Paper. Any chart paper which could be used for vertical line charts can be used for Equivolume charts, as long as the paper is not semi-logrithmic. We prefer to use a paper which is divided into eighths between each major division on the vertical axis. A division of tenths on the horizontal axis is handy when large volume days are being dealt with, but is by no means necessary. The paper which we like to use is printed by Reliance Chart Paper Company, 608 South Dearborn, Chicago, Illinois, and is their style "AS1." This is a large enough sheet (measuring 11 inches x 17 inches) so that about six months of market activity will fit on a sheet.

The Vertical Scale. The vertical scale used in a stock should be a function of the normal trading range of a stock, rather than merely its price. The chart paper mentioned above is divided into twenty parts on the vertical dimension, with each section divided into eighths. Ideally the stock should use most of this range during a six months period. Looking at past history will give a fairly good idea how much this stock is likely to fluctuate. On a low priced stock which does not move too

fast it would be advisable to allow two major divisions for each point. On a stock

in the twenty to sixty price range probably one point per major division is satisfact-

ory, but a very active and volatile stock in this price range may necessitate a less

sensitive scale such as one major division for each two points. High priced stock

will need a smaller scale such as two or four points per division.

It is important to arrive at a satisfactory scale for the price dimension. A

stock that moves fast enough to give wild gyrations on the chart had better be calmed

down by using a smaller scale or the charts will be extremely hard to interpret. On

the other hand, a scale that is not sensitive enough will tend to mask significant

stock action in a less volatile issue.

The Horizontal Scale. It is in the establishment of a horizontal scale that

the analyst must be especially careful. In order to properly analyze the action of

the stocks we are studying we must arrive at uniformity. Ideally, all of the stocks

we are studying will use the same number of columns in a given period of time. We

would like in this way to make a big day look the same in any stock, even though

in one stock 5,000 shares maybe exceptionally heavy trading, while in another issue

50,000 shares make up a very large day. In addition, we want to set a criterion for

a normal trading day, and have some way of recognizing days that are significant be-

cause of low volume. Sometimes the lack of volume is going to be just as important

as the presence of volume at other times.

The normal trading day, we have decided, should be represented by two columns on our charts. In that way a day with unusually light volume will show up with only one column while heavier trading days will occupy three or more columns. Therefore we will use about 260 columns in 130 trading days. One-half year of trading includes about 130 trading days, and there are 260 horizontal spaces on the chart paper we have suggested in the previous section.

In order to establish our scale, therefore, we must arrive at an average volume. Two or three months of history are sufficient to arrive at an average volume. Once having computed the average volume per day for the stock, we multiply this figure by .67 and then round off the answer to the nearest number which will be easily usable in our charting. Usually this will be a multiple of 5,000 shares.

Let us go through an example. A stock we wish to chart has had daily volumes as high as 120,000 shares and as low as 3,000 shares, but the average daily volume over the last three months has been 14,300 shares per day. Multiplying this number by .67 (this is the equivalent of taking two-thirds of it) we have 9,581. The nearest round number that we can easily work with is 10,000, so we will use that as our chart interval. In charting the stock we will use one column for each 10,000 shares or part thereof. Consequently a day on which the stock traded the average of 14,300 shares would occupy two columns on our chart. A day on which the stock traded exactly 20,000 shares would be charted two columns wide, but if the volume was 20,100 shares we would go to the third column. Any day on which 10,000 shares or less trade, the entry will only be one column wide.

Every stock will have its own average daily volume, but the principle is the same for any stock. A stock which trades an average of 80,000 shares a day, as a few do, will come up with a factor of 53,600 after multiplying by .67. The nearest usable number would be 55,000 shares, but would be more complicated than using 50,000 shares, and the difference between using 50,000 and 55,000 would hardly change our chart. Therefore we would be inclined to use the 50,000 interval for this stock. Therefore, any volume of 50,000 shares or less we would chart one column wide. A volume of at least 50,100 shares but not more than 100,000 shares would occupy two columns. 100,100 shares to 150,000 shares: three columns wide, etc.

The reader should realize that by setting different values for the horizontal scale, depending upon the stock, and determining the vertical scale by the volatility of the stock, all stock charts will look fairly similar. This is desirable. In order to set rules for the recognition of certain chart patterns we must have the patterns appear similarly, regardless of the price, volatility or volume of the stock.

Changes in Activity. Very often the characteristic volume of a stock will change. The traders will become interested in an issue, and a stock which usually trades about 2,000 shares a day will suddenly start to trade 30,000 shares a day, consistently. If this happens the chart section with the heavier volume will be very difficult to interpret, with a few days occupying large horizontal distances. The best thing to do in this case is to rechart the stock, using a new volume scale, based upon the heavier characteristic volume and not even use the chart section which represents trading prior to the abrupt increase in volume. It should be treated almost as though it were an entirely different issue.

Stock Splits. In vertical line charts a stock split, or a large stock dividend is compensated for by merely adjusting the price scale to show the new price. In Equivolume charting two adjustments must be made, one to the price and the other to the volume. If a stock normally trades 10,000 shares a day, and it is then split two for one, two things occur: the price is cut in half and the amount of outstanding stock is doubled. Since there is twice as much stock out, and its price is so much lower, the volume will obviously increase. In fact it will just about double. Therefore as soon as the stock starts to trade at the new price (not the when-issued stock) the volume increment should be doubled. In a stock with an average day of 10,000 shares, our horizontal scale would have been 7,500 shares, probably. After the split we would have a scale of 15,000 shares.

After the above two for one stock split we would also have to adjust the price. Since the stock is half the price it will probably be half as volatile. That is, if it was a $100 stock and normally traded in a three point range, it is now a $50 stock, and will trade in a one and one-half point range, since the percentage change will still be the same. Therefore, we must halve the vertical scale so that one and one-half points on the new section of the chart will look like three points on the old section. That is, if each major division on the old section of the chart represented two points, it will represent one point after the split.

Dating of Charts. Since each entry represents a day, there is little trouble in keeping track of time if occasional dates are entered on the chart. The easiest method is to note the first trading day of each month by a small entry near the margin of the chart. It is unimportant to us whether it was the first or the third of June when a stock hit its top, but we would like to know that a stock was at its high at approximately that date.

Dividends. As explained in Chapter IX, one type of gap which can occur in a stock is an ex-dividend gap. If we do not recognize the cause of the gap it may throw off our judgment. Consequently it is worthwhile, although not extremely necessary, to also note the ex-dividend days on the margin of the chart. This is more important if the stock pays a large dividend, an extra dividend or a stock dividend.

CHAPTER IV

TOPS

The two most important chart areas in a stock, from the standpoint of the trader are, of course, tops and bottoms. Properly recognizing and capitalizing on these chart areas is the surest way to stock market profits. Equivolume charting makes this recognition possible and therefore profitable.

Most books dealing with technical stock analysis do not talk about tops and bottoms; they talk about reversal areas. In addition, they define many different types of reversal areas such as "triangles", "rectangles" and "head and shoulders." We believe there is a basic fallacy to this sort of interpretation. It assumes that a stock, because it has completed an upward move, will begin a downward move, and vice versa. In actuality, there are three types of stock action: upward moves, downward moves and sideways moves. When a stock has completed an upward move, all we can be certain of from our charts is just that! The upward move is over. It is through going up, but is not necessarily ready to go down; it is much more likely to move sideways for some time, prior to changing again to another phase of market action. Even then it may move up rather than down after the sideways move is completed.

During an advance in a stock the upward force of demand is stronger than the downward force of supply. Prices are moving up because no long term equilibrium has been established in the stock. Buyers are anxious to acquire the stock, and are bidding prices higher. This finally ends when a lasting equilibrium is reached. There is enough stock being offered to satisfy the demand of the buyers without advancing the price of the stock. At this point in the stock the advance is at least temporarily over, but it does not mean, as most people seem to imagine, that the sellers are getting the upperhand and will force prices lower. As market analysts, and speculators, we can only feel certain that the advance has run its course. Later, there will be a move out of the horizontal pattern, but it could be either up or down, depending upon the balance between supply and demand at that time.

The trader who tries to recognize reversals in stocks usually will find himself in positions which take too long to develop. If he recognizes the end of an advance and therefore sells short, he may end up with a good profit when the stock goes down. If the stock moves sideways for a substantial period first, however, his money is inactive when it could be at work in another situation. In addition, it is very possible that the sideways move will be followed by another advance rather than a drop.

We recommend acting on only one market phase at a time. If an advance seems to have terminated the stock should be sold, but no short position should be entered into. If a sideways move develops, as would be expected, and then the stock makes a decisive move out of the sideways area, that is the time to establish a new position in the stock. People, and especially stock traders are likely to be impatient.

This leads to the tendency to think that stock movement consists of advances and declines. In reality, much of the time stocks are in sideways trends, where no profits of any consequence are available. It is necessary to force yourself to wait for moves to develop before making a commitment.

Patterns. Analysts have described many different types of market action that define the top of a stock, as mentioned in the previous section. We will not use any of these patterns, but we will, in this chapter, look at a few of them and relate them to Equivolume charting. It is true that patterns tend to repeat in the market, and at times they do look like a triangle or a rectangle. It is better, however, to realize that these patterns develop because of the interaction of supply and demand, and try to recognize the effect of these forces rather than categorize the patterns they often form on a chart. When a stock completes its upward move, supply and demand are at an equilibrium. The stock is likely to gyrate between fairly narrow limits as these two forces struggle for control. The result is a broadening top, which can appear in various ways, depending upon just how the supply and demand come in.

Tops in Equivolume Charting. In Equivolume charting we will generally be looking for a change from an upward move to a sideways move. The tipoff to this is an increase in volume accompanied by a narrowing of the spread. Other types of tops can occur, but this is the most important. This type of action will show itself as a day or a series of days in which the spread is narrow enough and the volume is heavy enough for the chart entry to be a square or even an "oversquare" day.

We will throughout this book refer to days in which a horizontal rectangle

is formed as an oversquare day rather than confuse it with the usual vertical rectangles that form during normal trading. An oversquare day is one in which prices
are able to move through only a very narrow price range, but a lot of stock changes
hands.

When a stock "goes square" it is meeting very heavy resistance. It is much
like a man who runs across a field, and then comes to a high strong fence. He may
push very hard against the fence but if it is strongly built he will not be able to go
beyond it. He will tend to get close to the fence, and push very hard, using much
more force than was necessary in running across the open field. Similarly, a stock
moves easily upward until it meets resistance in the form of stock being offered for
sale. If enough stock is being offered, no matter how hard they buyers try, they will
be unable to move the stock through the resistance area. In trying to get through the
resistance the buyers will move close to it and push hard. This shows itself in a narrow trading range and heavy volume.

Figure 4 is an example of this kind of action. The stock, Bethlehem Steel,
had been moving fairly easily throughout the month of January. On February third it
began to get far heavier volume, but still moved through a substantial range. The
next day it went quite square, and the following two days formed an oversquare pattern. In addition, the stock penetrated the ascending trend line across the bottoms
in late January. At this point it is obvious that supply has come in, and has overcome
the demand which brought about the move; the stock should be sold.

The reader will note that we combined two trading days in this analysis and

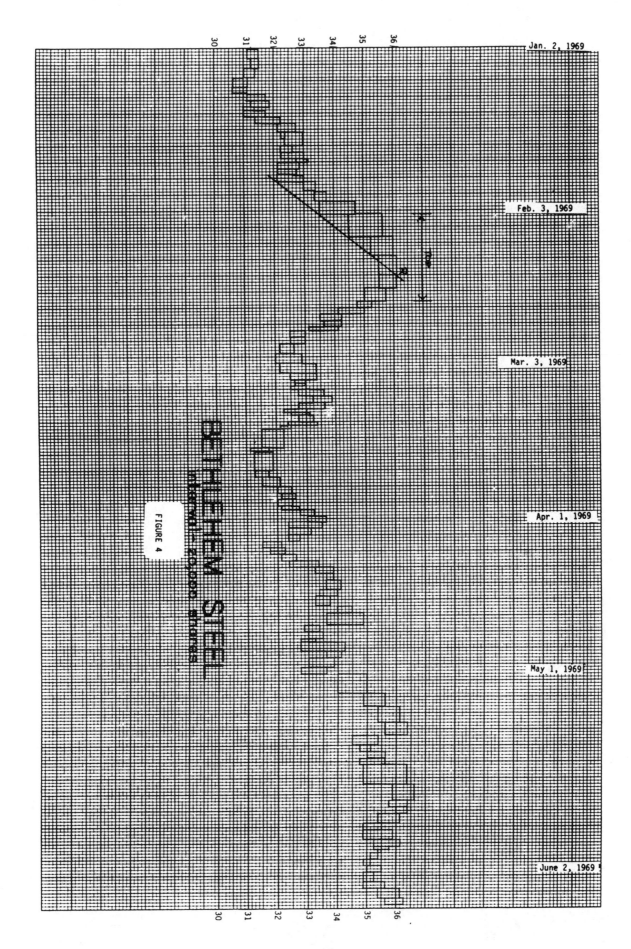

FIGURE 4

BETHLEHEM STEEL
interval- 20,000 shares

treated them as though they were one day. Since all we are concerned with is the balance between supply and demand this is legitimate. The market does not pay attention to trading days and neither should we. It happens in this case that the stock traded in the same range for two days before the supply became so heavy that prices started to be forced downward. Often we will combine many trading days in our considerations in order to properly interpret the forces of supply and demand.

An example of a stock which formed a top by combining many trading days is seen in Eastman Kodak in Figure 5. The stock never had a single very large volume day with a narrow spread but the entire month of May was occupied in trying to penetrate a resistance area just below $80. Combining the trading days we can see a flattening out of the stock. The fast advance which began in mid-April had run its course, and the trading days were becoming somewhat narrower, although no single day ever went square.

Occasionally a stock will move into a resistance area and trade huge volume without getting anywhere. This is such an obvious top that there is almost no way of missing it. Such trading can be seen in Fruehauf in Figure 6. Six trading days account for as much volume as more than a month of normal trading would. The breakout on a gap in early May brought in a great deal of buying, but there was obviously enough stock available to satisfy all buyers once the stock reached the 43-44 area. On a vertical line chart these six trading days would receive no more emphasis than any other days on the chart, but they are obviously significant. Using an Equivolume chart it would be almost impossible to miss the obvious signal that it was time to get

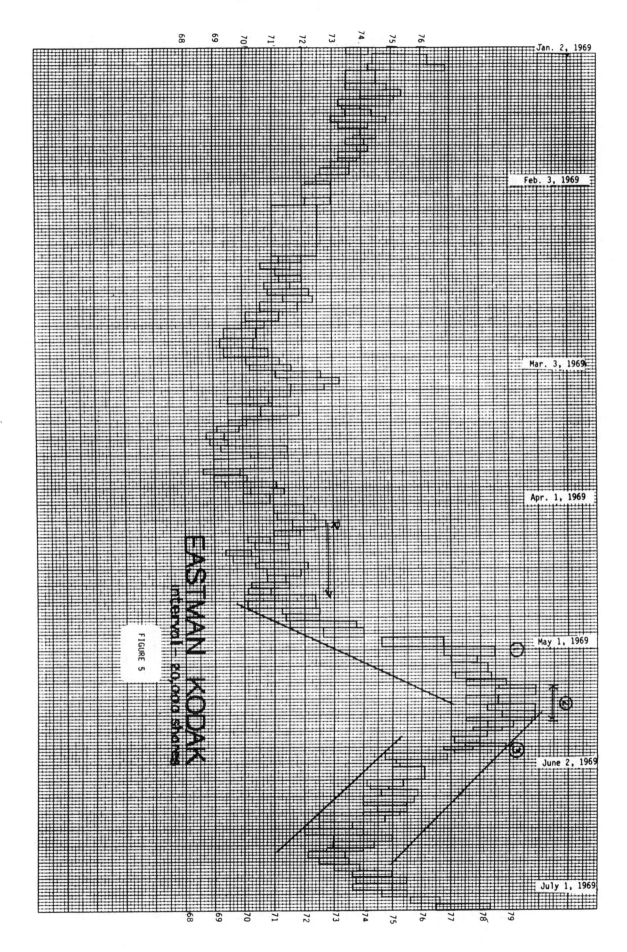

FIGURE 5

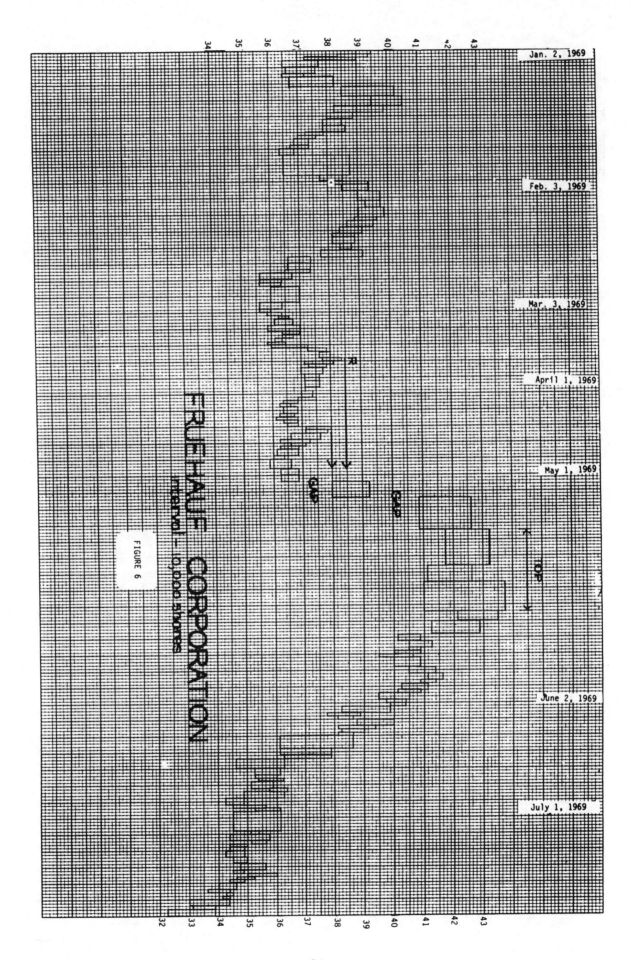

FRUEHAUF CORPORATION
interval— 10,000 shares

FIGURE 6

out of the stock.

Of course a stock does not always form a single peak as it reaches the end of a long advance. Often it takes two or three high points to complete the move. Gulf Oil, in April of 1969, is a good example of this sort of pattern (Figure 7). The stock reached 48 1/2 on heavy trading, but with a fairly wide trading range, so that the square type of formation did not show up. It then backed off for one day, only to rally again to 49 where it again met heavy supply. The following three days can then be grouped with this trading session, giving us an area of resistance which the stock appears to be unable to penetrate. Finally the stock moves down easily from this area, giving us a narrow day on the downside, and penetrating the ascending trend line. The next day is the final top before the decline. Here we see that the stock cannot even approach the old highs before again running into resistance. The day is a fairly square day, compared to adjacent trading days, and almost predicts the next day when the stock slides quickly downward.

As we have mentioned in two of the foregoing examples, penetration of a trend line is an additional indication that a top is being formed. A later chapter explains more thoroughly the use of trend lines, and should be reviewed in order to understand and recognize the end of an upward move.

Single Day or Two Day Reversals. Unfortunately a stock does not always go from an upward move to a sideways move in just the method illustrated in the previous section. Volatile stocks will sometimes culminate a move with a sudden upthrust and then a drop that is just as rapid. This can occur in one day, or two days.

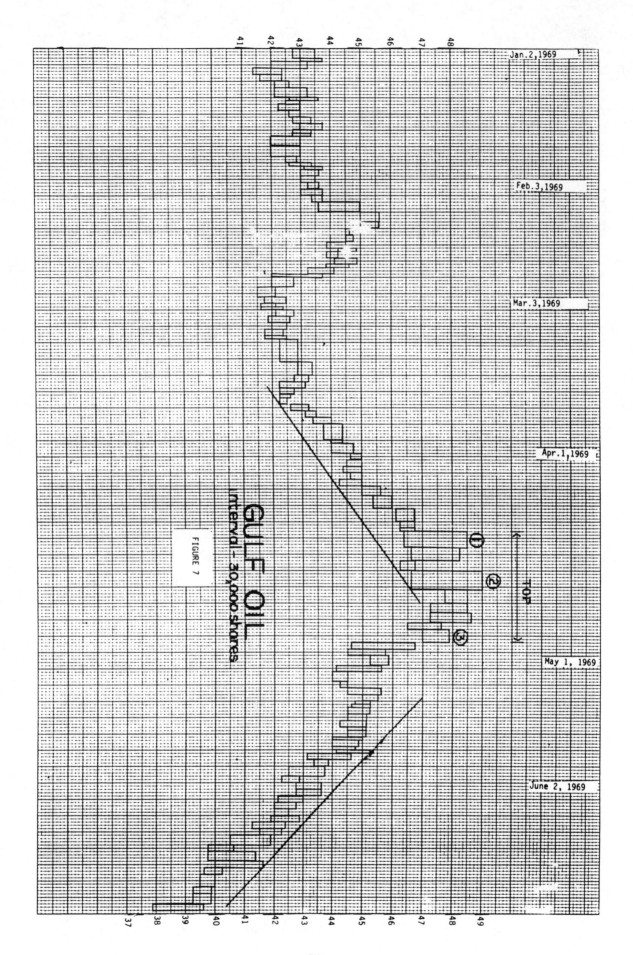

FIGURE 7

GULF OIL
Interval = 30,000 shares

If the action takes longer, it will appear as the tops we have been studying. The trading may be heavier than normal, but the spread will be wide enough so that they appear as normal rectangular days. Fortunately, this action is usually the first of a series of highs that make up a multiple top, so that you will usually get another chance to sell near the same levels. In fact the top in Eastman Kodak which we were studying in Figure 5 could be interpreted in this way. The first part of the top was a rapid upthrust and reversal which would have been extremely hard to interpret as a top. Later action, however, made the topping action fairly obvious. Often this type of topping is a part of a broad major top in a stock, with many tests of the highs.

The Head and Shoulders Top. One of the most widely referred to reversal formations is the head and shoulders. Figure 8 is an idealized head and shoulders as portrayed by a vertical line chart. It should, theoretically, have its highest volume on the left shoulder, lower volume on the head, and finally, even lower volume on the right shoulder. The idea is to wait until a stock has traced out this entire pattern, and finally penetrated the neckline after making the right shoulder before getting out of the stock. The trouble with this is obvious. You have left a good part of your profits behind if you wait that long, and your money has been tied up all the time the pattern was forming. In addition, when the stock is approaching the neckline after forming the right shoulder, there is still no certainty that the top has been formed until the neckline is actually penetrated. The downward move from here is usually rapid, and may cost you some more of your profits before you get out. We feel that it is more desirable to get out at the top of the head, and look for another

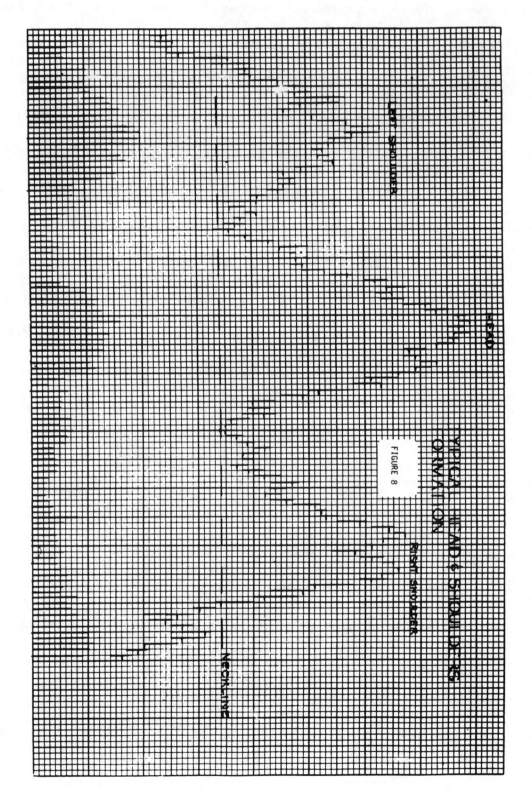

TYPICAL HEAD & SHOULDERS
FORMATION

FIGURE 8

stock to get into.

The head and shoulders top is actually nothing more than one of the many types of multiple tops that can form. The first top will usually have the heaviest volume, because the upthrust is then the strongest, and it will take a heavy supply to stop the move. Later, the subsequent tops will be formed on constantly decreasing volume as the buyers get weaker, and the advance is more easily thwarted.

Equivolume charting is ideal for dealing with the type of top which is often called a head and shoulders. The reason for this is the nature of these tops. The left shoulder is an upthrust and rapid reversal type of trading. The volume is heavy, but the trading range is almost always quite large. Therefore, the stock does not go square or oversquare on our charts as the left shoulder is formed, and we get no signal which says "get out." Therefore, we are kept in the stock until the second and higher peak, which is called the head.

Trading in the head area is usually not as heavy as in the left shoulder, but is still fairly heavy. A characteristic of the head is a rounding top with narrow spreads. In the head area we will get square days. We have our signal to get out, at the top of the move. After the head is formed the stock will trade downward, and usually penetrate the ascending trend line, giving us another chance to close out near the top. By the time the stock has formed the right shoulder and is deciding if it will penetrate the neckline we are long gone.

The top in American Telephone shown in Figure 9 is a very good example of a head and shoulders top. We would not have gotten out of long positions on the

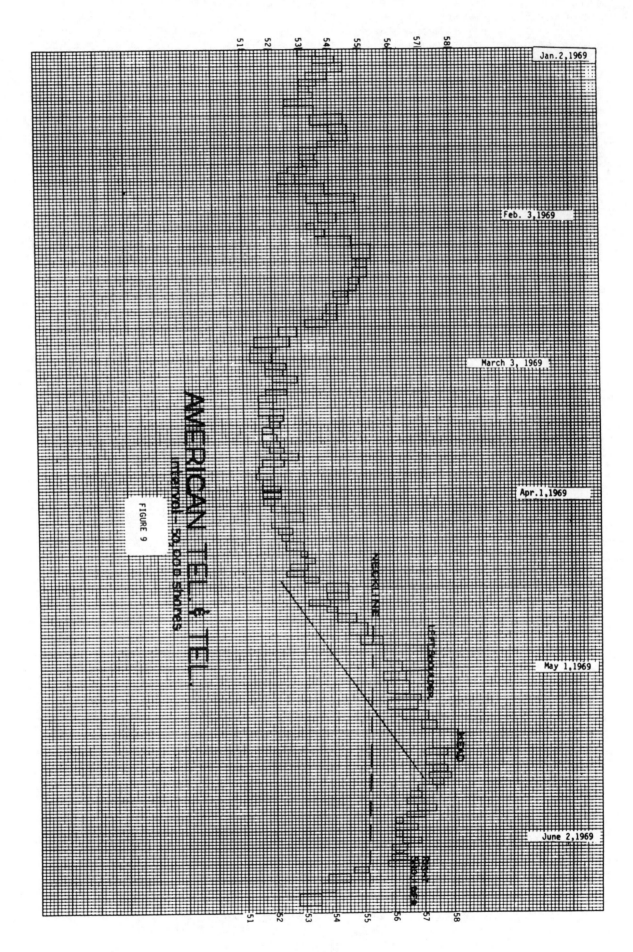

AMERICAN TEL. & TEL.
Interval—50,000 shares

FIGURE 9

first top at 57 1/8 because the stock had not gone square enough to alarm us. The next top at 58 1/8 is more square, however, and would probably cause us to sell. If we had not sold before then, certainly we would get out as soon as the ascending trend line was penetrated. This would have gotten us out of the stock somewhere between 56 3/4 and 58 1/8. The chartist who waited for a penetration of the neck-line could not have gotten better than 55 1/8 for his stock.

The Buying Climax. One type of top which is usually described by technicians is known as the buying climax. This consists of a very heavy volume, fast reversal, taking one or two days, and followed by the necessary "test" where prices return to their old highs on lighter volume before beginning to drop. In reality, there is no difference between this type of action and the multiple tops we have been discussing. In fact, it can be identical to the head and shoulders formation, if the test happens to slightly penetrate the old highs.

When a stock makes a quick reversal on heavy volume we get one or two large days which are still rectangles, and therefore do not tell us it is time to sell. The second move to these levels, after a small decline, almost always occurs on lighter volume (and, according to proponents of the buying climax analysis, must be on lighter volume). In addition, there is a tendency at this point for the spread to narrow. What we end up with, then, is a series of square or oversquare days, telling us it is time to get out.

As the reader should by now see, there are many names for the same type of market action. If a multiple top forms with the second top higher than the first top, analysts start calling it the right shoulder and head of a head and shoulders formation. If the second top comes in at about the same area as the first top they start calling it a buying climax and a successful test. If the second top is lower than the first top it begins to form either an equilateral triangle of a descending triangle, depending upon the low points being formed during topping. We shall deal more with triangles in the next section.

In discussing the buying climax, analysts point out that it is not a legitimate climax until it has been tested. This means that the stock must back away from its highs, and then approach them again. In order for a successful climax to occur, the test must be on lighter volume, and it must turn the stock back down. If the stock penetrates the old highs decisively, and volume becomes heavier, then the previous top was not a buying climax, but merely an intermediate top in a continuing uptrend.

In Equivolume charting the recognition is much easier. Whether or not the old highs are penetrated, of volume increases, or stays fairly high on the second rise and the stock moves upward with a wide spread, we have overcome a resistance area, and the stock is going higher. If the stock approaches the old highs and the spread narrows, showing heavy supply, and indicated by one or more days forming a square or oversquare condition, we have a sell signal. We don't have to try to decide whether we have a head and shoulder or a buying climax or any other picture on the chart. We can see that supply is getting too heavy, and we get out.

Triangles. Market technicians usually go to great lengths to describe the various types of triangles that form at the top of a move. Figure 10 illustrates these

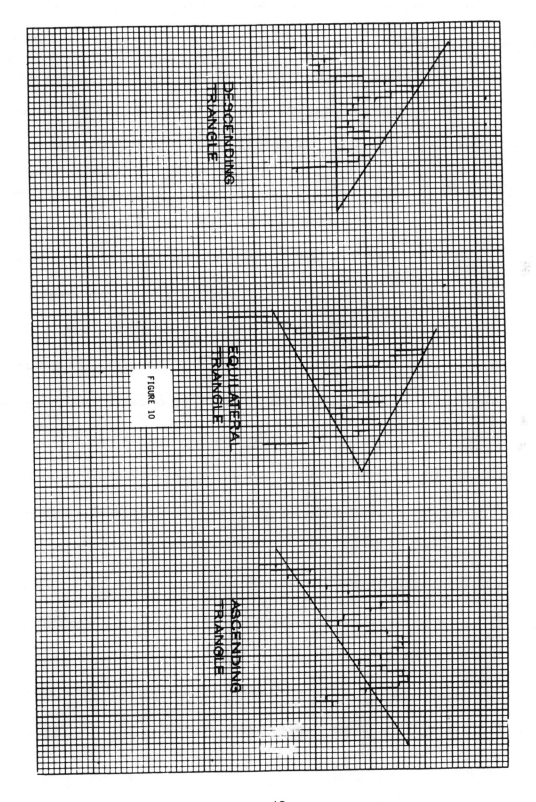

DESCENDING TRIANGLE

EQUILATERAL TRIANGLE

ASCENDING TRIANGLE

FIGURE 10

formations. It is interesting to note two factors, however, in studying charts which show these triangles. The first is that volume always decreases as the triangle forms, and the second is that the spread narrows on the tops of each return to the supply level after the first upthrust is completed. In other words, all tops act pretty much the same. If they are tops consisting of a number of highs, the first high will show up on Equivolume charts as rectangular days but the stock will go square on the subsequent tops.

When a stock is through going up it is not yet ready to go down. In fact it may take some time to slow down from its rapid upward move before starting to decline. The first approach to the resistance which is to eventually turn it down is done with much momentum, consequently the heavy volume and the large spread. The next approach to the same resistance is done with less momentum since the upward move has already been rebuffed once, therefore the somewhat lower volume but on a narrower spread. The stock may then try a number of times more to penetrate the resistance. If the resistance is strong enough the stock will finally succumb to the selling pressure and a downward move will develop. If the stock does penetrate the resistance on the upside we may be starting another advance, making the formation a consolidation rather than a reversal. If we go by our charts this is not a problem. We want to get out of our long positions when we recognize the beginning of a sideways move. It does not matter if it was a top or just a long consolidation; we should have already moved out of the position and be watching the stock to see what it is going to do after the sideways move is over. When it completes its move sideways and either penetrates the resistance or gives in to the selling we may want to

go back into the stock.

CHAPTER V

THE END OF A DECLINE

Having examined the action of stocks as they reach the top of an advance, we will now look at the similar circumstances as a stock completes a downward move. In reality, both actions are quite similar, and obey most of the same principles. There are some differences, however, which we will examine.

What we will be looking for, in this chapter, are areas where a stock finishes a downward move, at least temporarily. This does not necessarily mean that the stock will move up later. It may resume its decline after a sideways move. Our only concern is the temporary end of the selling which is at hand. Just as in tops, we are only interested in recognizing one market condition at a time.

There is only one reason for spotting the end of a decline. It is our opportunity to close out short positions. No other action should be taken when the end of a decline is recognized! When a stock is through going down, we can usually recognize it but all we do know is that the decline is over. We must wait for some further indication before taking a new position in the stock.

I doubt if any mistake is repeated more often in the stock market than the initiation of a long position upon recognition of the end of a decline. Everyone has the tendency to say "Wow – after that long drop the stock has finally quit going down and could run back up at least part way." It is an understandable and almost irresistible urge to immediately buy the stock. However, all we really know is that the decline has ended for the time being. A decline is followed almost invariably by a sideways move of some duration. Thereafter we will get another indication when the market starts a new move, either upward or downward. Although we have previously decided that we are unable to reach logical market conclusions based upon fundamentals, there are, nevertheless, fundamentals which have helped to cause the decline. It is not logical that the facts could change so radically and rapidly that a decline would immediately be replaced by an advance. It is much more likely that the selling would run its course, and be replaced by a basing action prior to a substantial advance. In fact, since a background of bad news evidently brought a-bout the decline it is very likely that the sideways action could then lead to more selling. In an extended bear market we have all seen stocks form very good bases after a decline, and then watched these bases be penetrated on the downside as the stocks searched for a new lower level of support. A declining market is usually ac-companied by selling climax after selling climax, at progressively lower levels.

Other books would have labeled this chapter "Bottoms." We are not really interested in bottoms, however. We are looking for the end of declines so that we can close out short positions, and put our money to work in another situation. Only time will tell us whether it was in fact a bottom, or a consolidation area in a con-tinuing down trend. The next chapter will explain the recognition of the end of a sideways move. It is then that we will want to initiate new positions. Why buy a stock when the decline appears to be over? At best, we are likely to have a long wait before the stock starts back up, and at worst, the subsequent move may be down rather than up. In fact, the odds favor the latter. For every legitimate turning point there are many sideways consolidations which are not a reversal of trend.

The idea is to trade signal to signal. Trying to call the turns can be very tempting, but it can also be disastrous!

The Sellout. As in the formation of tops, the indication of lows is volume. There is more likelihood in the formation of a base, though, for the first bottom to be climactic. That is, it will consist of heavy volume, but on a wide spread rather than a narrow spread, and will be a quick down and then up action. The result is one or two heavy volume, but rectangular, days. This is the sellout phase of the decline, and is usually a reliable indication that the stock is going from "down" to "sideways." What has happened is that sellers have been driven to the point where they are willing to sell at any price, just to get out. The stock has dropped rapidly to the point where substantial demand has been waiting. At this level buyers have put a bottom on the stock and force it upward again quickly, not wishing to miss the bargain prices. With the exhaustion of this demand, however, the rally usually soon runs out of steam. Those people who have not sold before see a chance to sell at a little better price, and force prices down toward the old lows. Volume is lower, however, with the large professional traders having done their buying on the previous decline.

The Test. As prices approach the old lows, or even penetrate them, volume and spread become very important. The volume is likely to increase, and the spread to narrow, giving us square or over-square trading days. This is certainly a confirmation that it is time to buy in the stock we were short. The subsequent rise from these levels will usually penetrate the descending trendline also. If we cover our shorts on the first high volume decline and rally, we are likely to cover at a price somewhat above the lows, since the rally is usually very rapid, and not recognized on our charts until it is well underway. In addition, there is a good chance that the test will be unsuccessful and that the stock will move lower. Therefore, it is best to wait for the test, and if it is a successful test, where the days go square, then cover short positions.

Bottoms, if they turn out to be bottoms, are usually made up of many returns to the lows, forming a broad base, and giving us plenty of time to act. Therefore it is not very dangerous to wait for the test after we recognize a climax. The stock is not likely to run away on the upside, with us still holding our short positions. Very often the rally which follows the first low is referred to by the tape watchers as a short covering rally. This it may be, but we do not recommend it for our short covering. There will probably be another chance to cover the shorts, and at a better price.

Bottom Formations. Most of what was said in the previous chapter about top formations can be equally applied to bottom formations. The fact that they often look like a head and shoulders, a triangle or a square need not concern us. For one thing, by the time it starts to form a recognizable picture we will, hopefully, be trading in another stock. There is no more reason to be trapped in a long sideways move after a decline than there was to do the same thing after an advance.

Just as in tops, the formation of a bottom consists of a narrowing of trading as the stock tries to penetrate the old lows. This manifests itself in heavy trading as the stock approaches the support area, and a narrowing spread. It also shows up as a steady decrease in volume across the entire formation.

The result can very easily be a triangle, since the stock is trying to penetrate a support at a given level, and each rally is likely to be weaker. The triangle is not an indication, however. The way in which the stock trades, in terms of volume and spread is our indication of the location and strength of the support. In all bottoms, as in all tops, it is entirely a case of the interaction of supply and demand. The patterns which may form are a manifestation of those forces.

Examples. Figure 11 shows a typical end to a decline. After hitting a high in mid-February, Loews Theaters declined rapidly from 61 all the way to 39 5/8 where it met support on heavy volume, with a wide spread. After the rally to 44 1/2 it sank back to the old lows, again on heavy volume, but this time with a narrower spread. It had hereby indicated the end of the decline, and the beginning of a sideways move. After another test of the lows with still lighter volume in the first week of April, the stock tried to advance but met heavy resistance just below 50. As can be seen, when the stock finally broke out of the 40-50 area it was a breakout on the downside rather than the upside. The trader who had taken the bottom as a buy signal would probably have held through the various rallies, and ended up with a loss, after having his money tied up from the beginning of May until the end of June.

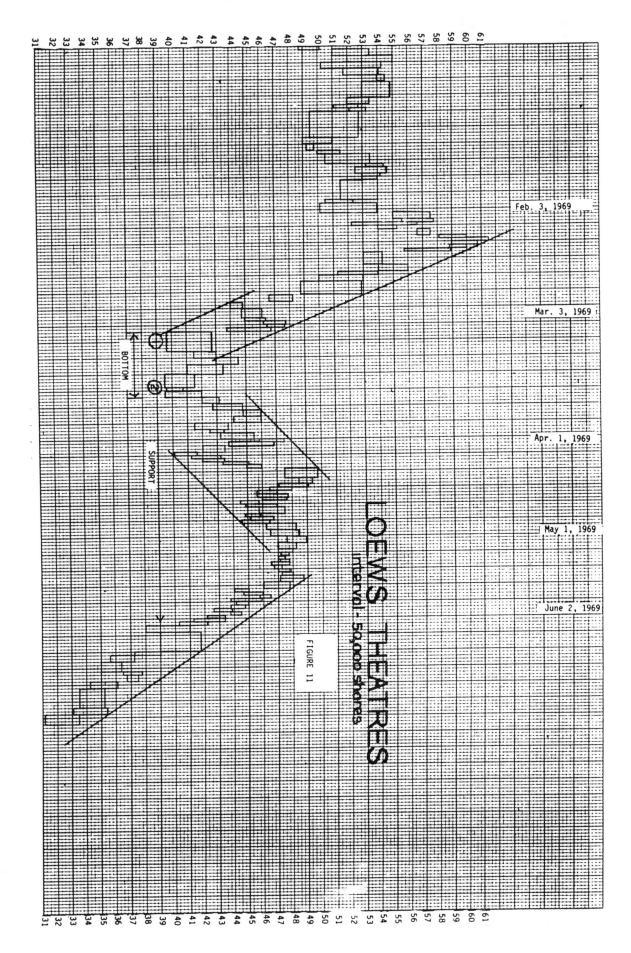

LOEWS THEATRES
Interval-50,000 shares

FIGURE 11

Feb. 3, 1969

Mar. 3, 1969

Apr. 1, 1969

May 1, 1969

June 2, 1969

BOTTOM

SUPPORT

Of course, there was room for a profit by buying on the lows, and selling at the top of any of the rallies, while the stock was in a generally sideways move. This is fine for a nimble trader, and can be very profitable. The end of the rally in the 50 area followed exactly what we would expect, as delineated in the previous chapter, and would have gotten us out. The longer term investor should not follow this practice, however. Even though the charts tell us that the decline has ended, the odds still favor a later resumption of the decline, rather than a reversal to a bullish chart pattern.

According to the Elliot Wave Theory, any advance is likely to be comprised of three separate upward moves, interrupted by two sideways moves. The same pattern also holds for major declines. Consequently, for each true bottom or top there are two sideways moves that are only pauses in a continuing trend. Obviously, then, if we try to pick the top or the bottom of a move, our chances are only one in three of being right!

The chart of Pepsico (Figure 12) is another example of a bottom. We see here a heavy volume, wide rectangular day which certainly looked like a selling climax, in the last week of February. Once again, this was followed by a rally, and then a test of the lows. Note that the second low was done on even heavier volume, and was slightly below the previous low. The indication that a bottom was indeed forming was the narrower spread. The stock was meeting good support, and was going more square. The next decline penetrated the old lows, but on light volume, and should not in any way have changed our thinking. Shorts should have been closed out on

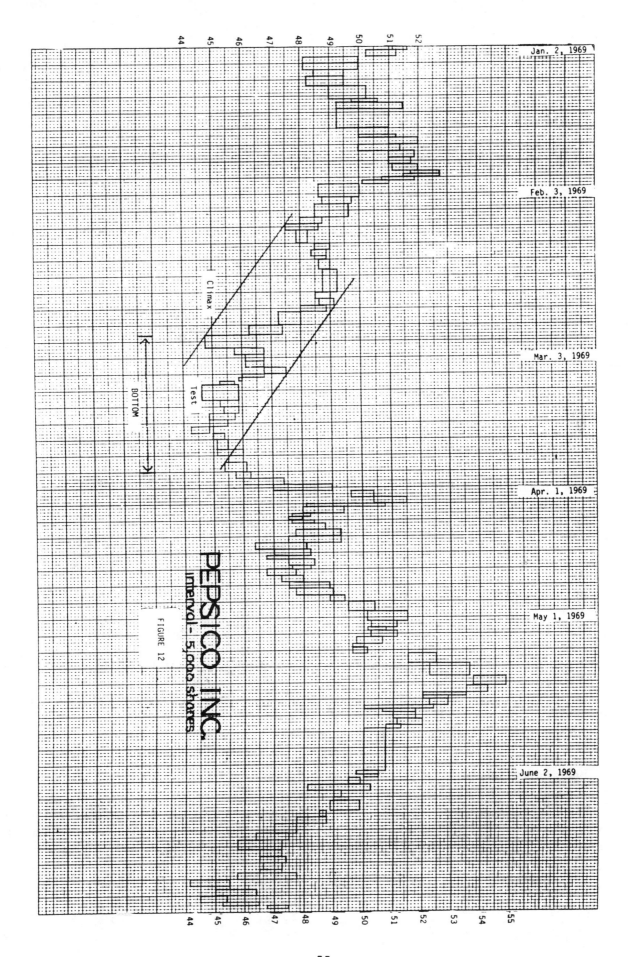

PEPSICO, INC.
Interval – 5,000 shares

FIGURE 12

Jan. 2, 1969

Feb. 3, 1969

Mar. 3, 1969

Apr. 1, 1969

May 1, 1969

June 2, 1969

one of these base days.

Occasionally a stock will form a very noticeable base, trading huge volume, and going oversquare. Such is the case in Chrysler in Figure 13. In three days Chrysler traded as much stock as it normally would trade in twenty or more days. These days were all quite square, and grouped together give a very oversquare pattern. There could be little doubt that the stock had met with a very substantial area of support. After a long decline the stock had gapped downward as selling poured in. Evidently, however, there were buyers ready to acquire all offered stock at the 24 level.

The reader will note that the same type of activity occurred earlier in the stock, and it did in fact lead to a rally, but the stock soon resumed its downward move after the stock penetrated this support area.

Finally, let us look at the bottom formed from late July until early September in General Motors (Figure 14). General Motors is a very widely held and actively traded stock. In fact, it trades so heavily that we have to use a 50,000 share volume interval for it. As a consequence, there is less variation in the width of days than there would be in a more volatile stock. We become much more dependent upon the size of the trading ranges in analyzing this stock. What told us that the decline had been halted was the narrowing of the spread from the first low to the second low, and again at the third low. An additional signal was given when the stock gapped through its descending trend line after rising from the third bottom. Even this only tells us that the decline has at least temporarily ended. The penetration of the trend

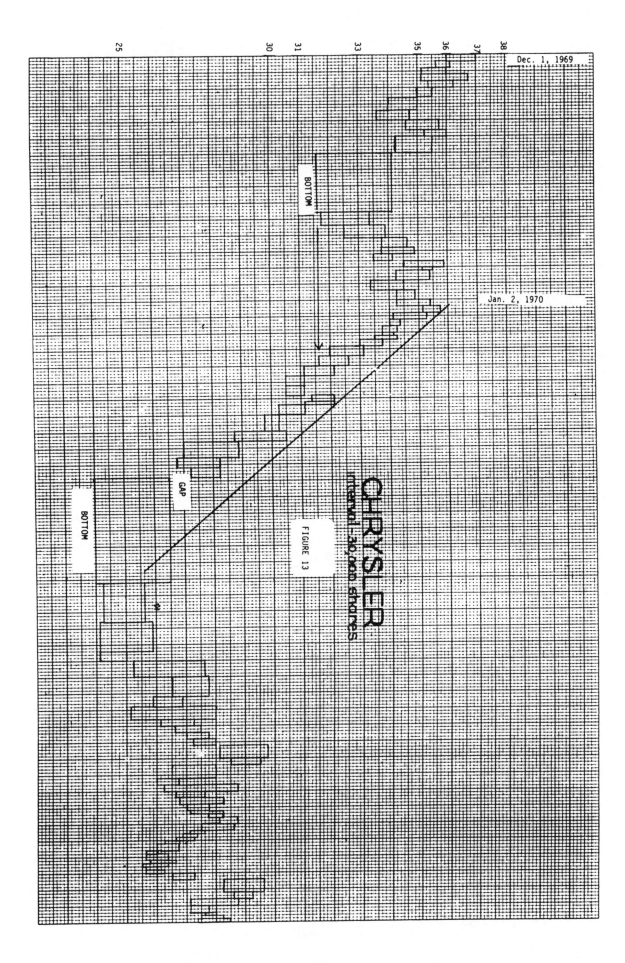

CHRYSLER
internal 30,000 engines

FIGURE 13

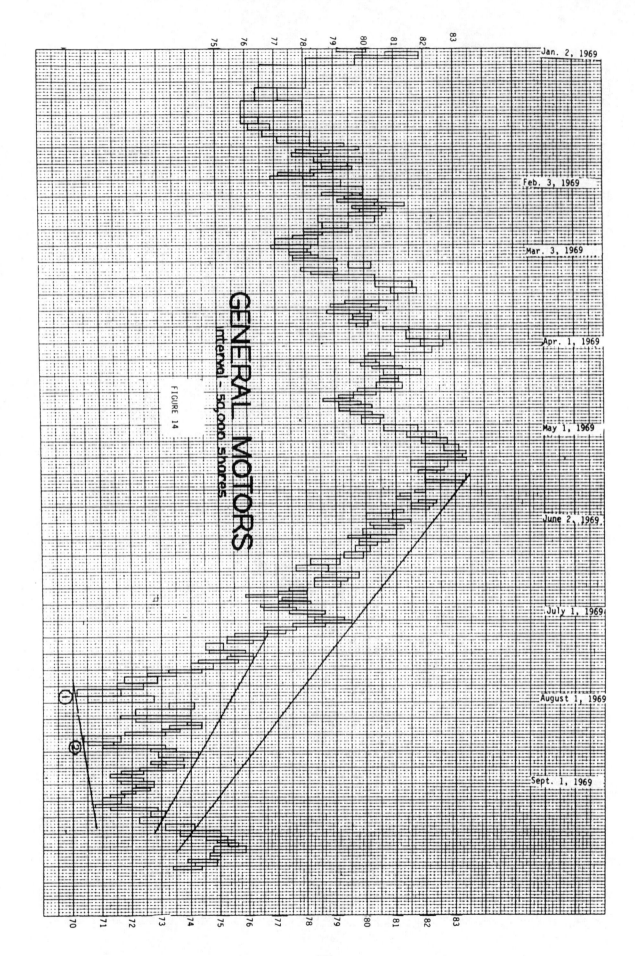

GENERAL MOTORS
Interval – 50,000 shares

FIGURE 14

Jan. 2, 1969
Feb. 3, 1969
Mar. 3, 1969
Apr. 1, 1969
May 1, 1969
June 2, 1969
July 1, 1969
August 1, 1969
Sept. 1, 1969

line is not a new signal which tells us to buy, it just confirms the end of the decline.

In general, bottoms are more difficult to recognize than tops. They obey the same general rules, however. The next chapters will tell the reader how to recognize opportunities to buy or sell. Tops and bottoms are meant only for closing out established positions.

CHAPTER VI

CONSOLIDATION FORMATIONS

Consolidation formations and their completion are the most important aspects of technical analysis for the investor following the methods outlined in this book. They provide the timing for the buying or short selling of stocks. As we have shown in the two previous chapters, no new commitment should be made at the end of an upward or downward move. The time to initiate a new position is at the beginning of a move rather than at the beginning of a sideways consolidation.

After a stock completes an upward or downward move it usually gives a fairly obvious signal that the move is over. After this, the stock will move sideways for some time. As we will see in the chapter dealing with targets, the extent of this sideways move is important in judging the probable extent of the subsequent upward or downward move. There are various typical formations during this move which we will look at individually in this chapter. They are usually best expressed as geometrical patterns, but our primary emphasis will be upon the volume during these sideways moves, and their consequent appearance on Equivolume charts.

Our aim throughout this chapter will be to establish methods for the recognition of the termination of sideways moves. Only in this way can we recognize opportunities to go long or short.

Figure 15 is a chart of National Dairy Products in the first half of 1969. It shows quite clearly the tendency of stocks to intersperse market moves with sideways consolidations. The reader can see in this example that there is no indication at the beginning of each consolidation as to the direction of the subsequent move. He can also see that there appears to be a relationship between the extent of the sideways move and the extent of the later upward or downward move.

Triangles and Rectangles. Two types of consolidation generally occur in a consolidation area, triangles and rectangles. These can be of various types, and will be individually discussed and illustrated. It is worthwhile first to differentiate between these two main categories, however. A rectangular consolidation takes place when there are well defined areas of support and resistance in the stock. At approximately the same price the stock always receives support, and above these levels is an area at which it runs into resistance. There is a standoff between supply and demand. There is no way of knowing which way the stock will move out of this area, and it is hard to determine when it is likely to.

On the other hand, triangles of any sort represent a constant change in either supply or demand, or both. If the bottom is rising while the top remains horizontal, supply is constant, but demand is getting stronger. If the tops are declining and the bottom is horizontal, supply is increasing, and sellers are willing to get out at progressively lower prices, while buyers are holding their ground, and waiting for the sellers to come to them. Triangles are reflecting change, while rectangles are re-

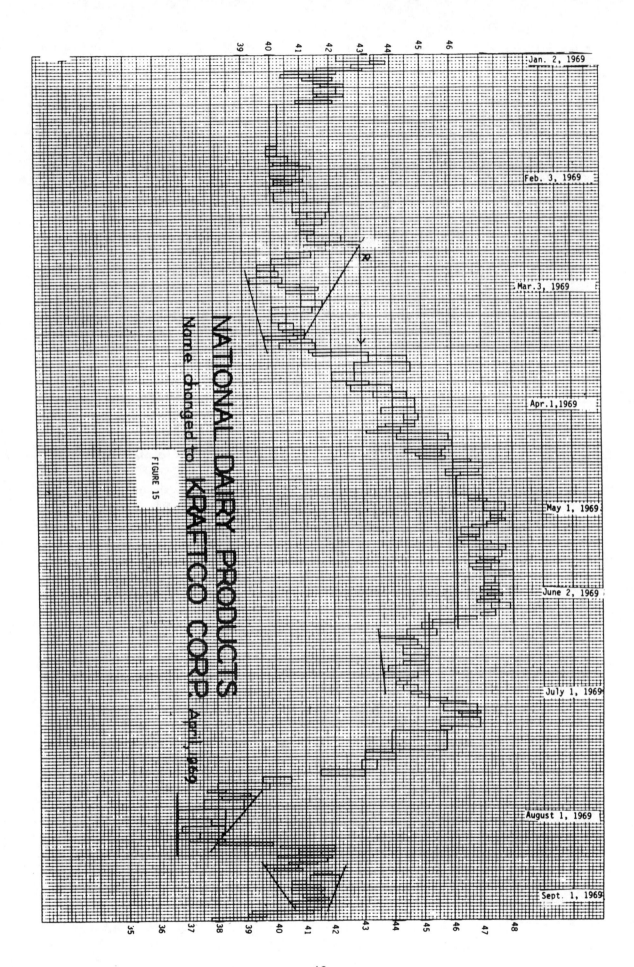

NATIONAL DAIRY PRODUCTS
Name changed to KRAFTCO CORP. April, 1969

FIGURE 15

Jan. 2, 1969

Feb. 3, 1969

Mar. 3, 1969

Apr. 1, 1969

May 1, 1969

June 2, 1969

July 1, 1969

August 1, 1969

Sept. 1, 1969

flecting stability. Triangles provide us with more information, since we are interested in interpreting the change in investor sentiment. For this reason they are somewhat more valuable as a predictive tool.

Volume Across a Consolidation. It is safe to say that almost all consolidations are accompanied by a decrease in volume as they progress. They generally start with heavy volume, as traders are still expecting a continuation of movement. As time progresses the traders see that the stock has started to go sideways, and they move to other issues for their excitement. Volume then continues to dry up until something happens to change the situation. It is our intention to recognize this drying up of interest, and do nothing in the stock until there is an indication that the sideways move has terminated. When the stock tells us that the consolidation is over, and a new move is starting we will either buy the stock or sell it short, depending upon the direction it has indicated it will move.

Volume is the most important indicator of the end of a consolidation, just as it was the indication of the end of a rise or decline. In conjunction with the spread it tells us that the situation has changed. The traders are again coming into the stock, and initiating a new move, either upward or downward.

Rectangles. The most common type of consolidation is a rectangle. The stock, after terminating a move then is bracketed by sellers above and buyers below. The price of the stock moves between these two levels rebounding from the demand on the downside, and retreating from the supply on the upside. The result is a holding of the stock between two horizontal or nearly horizontal limits.

CONSOLIDATION FORMATIONS

The difficulty with rectangles is that their extent cannot be ascertained. The stock can stay between these limits for a long time unless something upsets the supply and demand balance. The trader must be careful not to have his money tied up in such a situation, since his capital will be idle until the breakout, and it may be a long time before it occurs. In addition, there is no way of knowing in which direction the breakout will occur. Since the stock is being held between horizontal limits, the buyers and sellers are equally strong. As we have stated in the previous chapter, if the sideways move comes after a decline, regardless of what type of sideways move it is, the odds favor a continuation of the decline. The sideways move, when rectangular, does not give us any further indication of the probable move until it terminates.

The rectangular consolidation has its advantages, however. The breakout, when it does occur, is very reliable. It is very rare that it indicates an up move and then does not continue it. In addition, the support and resistance area are well defined, making the breakout easy to recognize.

As a rectangular consolidation takes place the stock will tend to move easily between the support and resistance areas, and tend to go square at the extremes of each swing. In addition, days will tend to get narrower, but also have smaller spreads as the move progresses across the chart. The breakout takes place by the stock approaching the resistance, but instead of going square, penetrating the resistance. The breakout is usually done on heavier volume, and is most reliable when this occurs. The most important sign, however, is a widening of the spread. Increasing volume with a narrowing of the spread, as we have previously pointed out represents the triumph of the resistance area. On the other hand, increasing volume with a widening of the spread represents the defeat of the resistance area. A stock that moves through the top of a consolidation rectangle with a wide spread is telling us that something new is happening in the stock. The factors which were holding in the sideways area have been overcome, and demand is now more powerful than supply.

If a stock moves through a resistance area, and volume is very heavy, with a narrow trading range, causing a square day, the move is suspect. The stock has evidently found a new supply area just above the old one. At best, the stock is likely to pull back either to the top of the old trading range or even return to it. At worst, it may be a short-lived rally which will then be followed by a penetration of the consolidation area in the other direction. The analyst should remember that volume in itself is not enough. It must be accompanied by a good wide spread in order to be a reliable indicator.

Pullbacks. After a stock has moved through a resistance area the subsequent move is still not likely to be immediate. Unless the stock is extremely strong it will have utilized much of its momentum in penetrating the resistance. It is normal at this point for it to pull back on light volume. The pullback is typified by narrow days, with fairly wide spreads, giving "normal" rectangular days on the Equivolume chart. The pullback is most likely to stop at the top of the old rectangle. If the stock pulls back to this area and then starts to go square it is an excellent time to make a commitment. A very strong stock may not pull back at all, however, so the more aggressive investor is advised to go in as soon as he recognizes the breakout, with the intention of holding through the pullback if it occurs. If the stock appears to be pulling back, but then goes far enough to penetrate the bottom levels of the old rectangle, the stock should be immediately sold.

Bull and Bear Traps. As mentioned before, if the breakout is too square, there is a danger that it may not be a legitimate move. In addition, if a stock moves through a resistance area out of a rectangular formation, and volume is unusually light, indicating that it cannot gather a following, the move is also suspect. There is evidently no power to the move, and little likelihood of a substantial follow-through. This is known as a trap. If it is on the upside it is a bull trap; if it is on the downside it is a bear trap. Volume and spread are the indicators of a trap. Either unusually light volume, indicating lack of strength, or a narrow spread, indicating heavy resistance, should be a warning. The speculator who is overly wary of traps is better off than one who does not look for them. There are plenty of stocks to trade, and breakouts occur all the time. It is better to concentrate on the ones which meet our criteria; an increasing volume with a widening spread. You may miss some good opportunities but you are less likely to get caught. In addition, it should be repeated: If you find yourself in a trap it will be signaled by a penetration of the other side of the previous rectangle. It is imperative that the position be immediately closed out! In fact, this is such a strong signal that the speculator would be well advised not only to close out the position, but reverse it.

All of the foregoing principles show up very clearly in the action of General Dynamics in Figure 16. The stock was moving between 45 1/2 and 48 throughout the

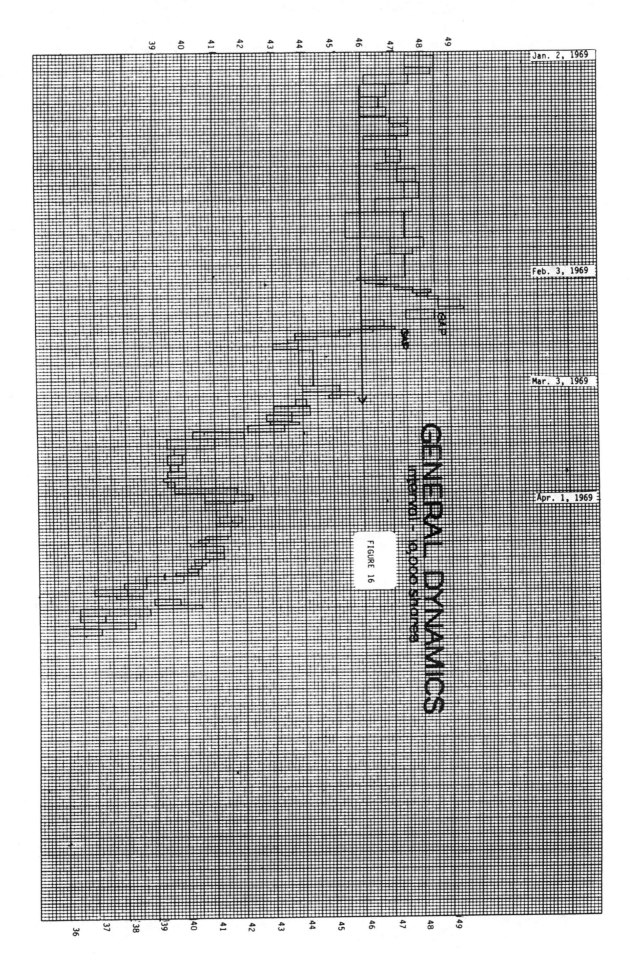

FIGURE 16

GENERAL DYNAMICS
Interval – 10,000 shares

Jan. 2, 1969

Feb. 3, 1969

Mar. 3, 1969

Apr. 1, 1969

month of January. The extremes tended to be square, indicating resistance. In early February the stock moved to 49 1/2 on light volume. The lack of volume and spread were signaling a bull trap. The speculators who were watching for a breakout could easily have jumped in on this move. The reversal was rapid, however, with two gaps on the way down. When the stock moved through the bottom of the resistance it was moving easily. Volume was not heavy, but the spread was large. There was no resistance to the move until the stock got down to 43 where it went square, then pulled back to 45 3/4. This is just below the bottom of the old rectangle. The reversal from this area completes the formation. The stock appears destined to go lower, and the wise speculator should be short the stock.

Equilateral Triangles. Closely related to the rectangle is the equilateral triangle. Again, we have an equal strength of supply and demand. That is, the buyers are not any more anxious than the sellers, so we have no indication of the ensuing move. In the case of the equilateral triangle, however, the sellers are dropping their asking prices as time goes by and the buyers are raising their bids. The result is a narrowing toward an apex, at which time a move is likely to start. One advantage to the triangle over the rectangle is that the speculator can have some idea how long he has to wait before there will be some action.

Usually a stock will actually break out before the apex is reached. In fact, a stock which reaches the apex of the triangle is likely to then just drift along sideways in a narrow range, with light volume. A breakout when the stock is still a long way from the apex is very reliable. A breakout near the apex is unreliable, and should not be acted upon. As in rectangles, the same rules hold true. Look for a wide spread, and watch for a moderate increase in volume to accompany the move. Traps are not as likely out of an equilateral triangle, but they do happen.

Right Triangles. Right triangles are an extremely common and very reliable formation. As the name implies, they have one sloping trend line and one horizontal trend line. In a stock which is in an advance, the common type of triangle is a right triangle which has an upward sloping series of lows, and a firm horizontal series of tops. The stock is meeting a resistance area, and is more and more closely approaching it, but is unable to penetrate it. It remains to be seen if the stock can get through the resistance. Since it was in an upward move, the odds of course favor the resumption of the move. Hence a triangle is most likely to be penetrated through its horizontal trend line. A penetration of the sloping line would have to be a change of direction.

As in rectangles and equilateral triangles, the clue is in the spread. A valid penetration must be made on a widening spread, and is likely to be stronger if it is accompanied by increasing volume. When a breakout from a right triangle occurs, and it meets these criteria, the trader should immediately make a commitment. There is much less likelihood of a pullback from a right triangle than from a rectangle, so there may be no second chance.

Right triangles are generally a continuation formation rather than a reversal formation, so the trader is better off if he only moves on breakouts from triangles that act as they should and are a continuation of an established trend. When a stock reverses its direction it is most likely to do it from a rectangle. Figure 17 shows the

way in which various types of consolidation patterns appeared in Royal Dutch Pet-

roleum. First we see, in early January, the formation of a descending right triangle

which is penetrated on the upside by a rectangular day. This evidences easy move-

ment, and assures us that the move has further to go. The advance ends with two quite

square days, and the stock starts to move sideways. Since each decline goes a short-

er distance, the formation becomes an ascending right triangle. The upside resistance

at 52 7/8 is penetrated when the stock moves to 53 1/4, but the squareness of the two

days shows heavy upside resistance, and the stock soon drops out of the triangle on

the downside with an increase in volume and a widening of the spread. The stock

had signaled a downward move. Upon returning to the old support area at 48 the

stock again shows that it is entering a consolidation area. This develops into a rec-

tangle. Note that the heavy volume bottom is formed with a wide spread, but the

level is later tested on lighter volume, and the trading is much more "square." There

is no mistaking the breakout from the rectangle. The volume gets heavier, and the

stock moves from 49 1/2 to 51 1/8 in one day.

Flags and Pennants. All of the formations which we have discussed up until

now are of fairly long duration, and are preceded by a sign that a sideways move is

developing. These are times when we should be watching, but should have no posi-

tion in the stock. As a stock progresses through either an advance or a decline, how-

ever, there are other pauses which do not require our getting out of the stock. They

are resting places during the move. Their formation is quite similar to the triangles

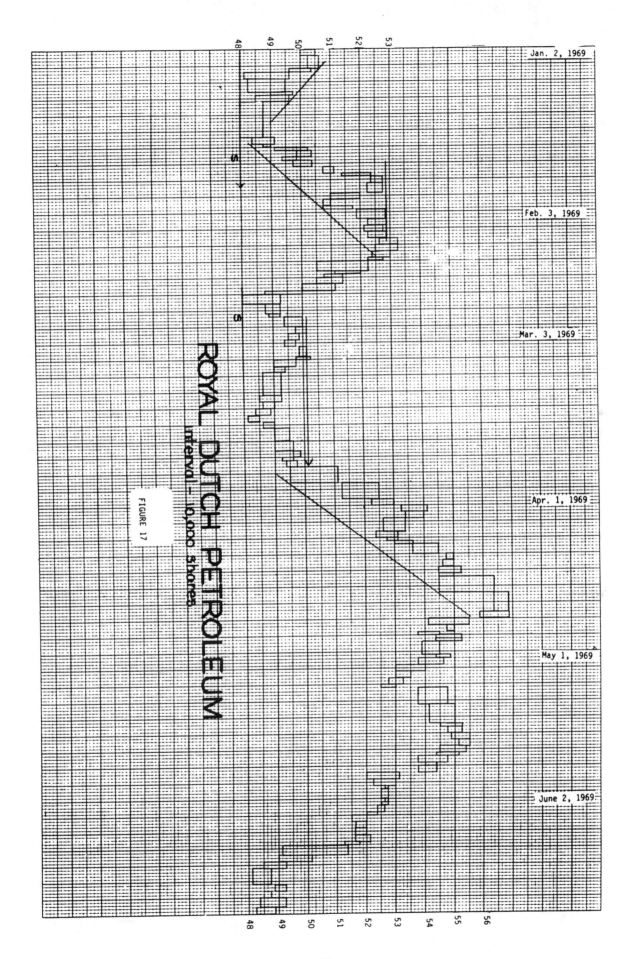

ROYAL DUTCH PETROLEUM
Interval = 10,000 shares

FIGURE 17

Jan. 2, 1969
Feb. 3, 1969
Mar. 3, 1969
Apr. 1, 1969
May 1, 1969
June 2, 1969

and rectangles we have already discussed, but they are of much shorter duration.

The distinguishing characteristic of this sort of pause, as compared to the longer formations is that they are not preceded by an indication that the move is over. The stock starts to go sideways after an advance without indicating that a top has been formed. If there is any buildup of volume prior to the sideways move, it does not come in conjunction with the characteristic narrowing of the spread. If it is a pause in a downward move it does not follow climactic selling.

These formations are reliable in that they indicate that the move has further to go. A stock which is moving up strongly would, without these intermediate resting points, quickly become overbought, and would then put in a major topping formation. The small sideways corrections on the way up gradually get the scared sellers out, and keep the move going. A strong move that does not incorporate small sideways moves should be considered dangerous. When the move is over, it will terminate rapidly and decisively, perhaps allowing little time to get out near the highs. A healthy move is one that digests selling as it progresses. The same principles are of course true in a decline. The buyers and short coverers must be accomodated during the decline in order for the move not to run out of momentum.

These formations usually are accompanied by a decreasing in volume as they progress, so that the days get narrower as the move runs its course. Although this narrowing does show up in Equivolume charts, and would not in vertical line charts, in other respects these formations look much as they would on vertical line charts. There are two normal formations. One is the flag. In this formation the prices drop away from the prevailing trend, and the tops and bottoms are parallel. In the second

formation, the pennant, the stock starts to go horizontally, but there is a converging

of the tops and bottoms, producing a figure that does look like a pennant. Hecla

Mining, in Figure 18 shows various consolidations during its decline in early 1969.

Besides a flag in early March and a pennant which formed in mid-April, the stock

gave a signal of an end to the decline in early May, and formed a typical triangle,

which was then penetrated on the downside two weeks later.

Similar formations, this time on the upside can be seen in First Charter Fin-

ancial in Figure 19. In early August the stock formed a good flag, and later in the

month it formed a pennant.

Other Patterns. In addition to the foregoing consolidation patterns there are

many variations. These are often treated separately, but in reality are only modi-

fications of the same patterns. If a right triangle on the upside forms, but the stock

is particularly strong, the upper limits will be an upsloping line rather than a hori-

zontal line. Consequently, the pattern will be an uptrending wedge. The rules are

the same, however. It will be terminated by a penetration of the pattern on a widen-

ing spread, giving a long, narrow day.

If a stock is moving through a rectangular formation, but the forces are par-

ticularly strong on the sell side, the pattern may be two parallel but downtrending

lines rather than two absolutely horizontal lines. The only difference is that the

stock has given an additional indication of its weakness in that the rectangle is it-

self a weak one.

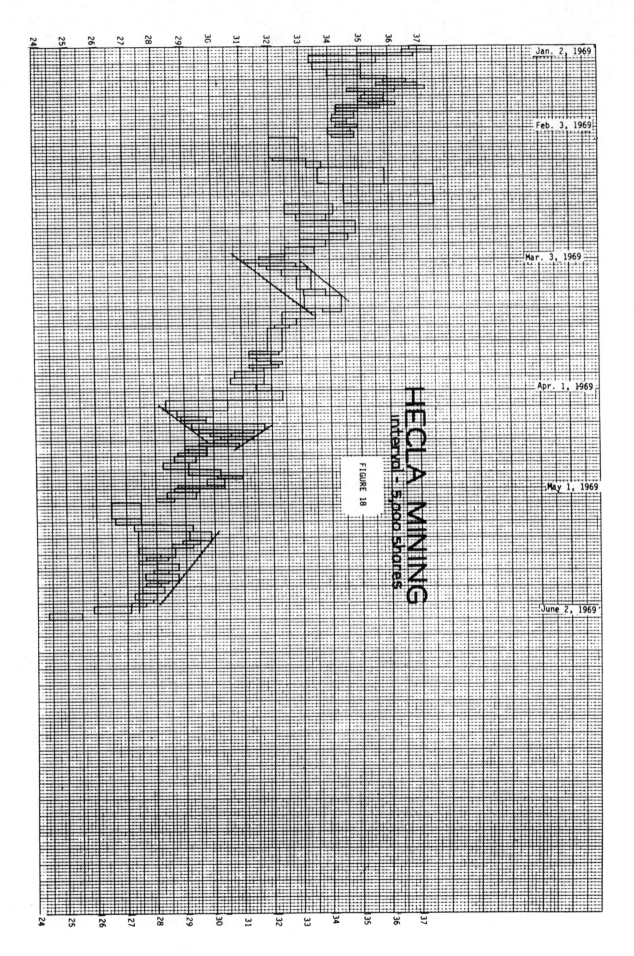

FIGURE 18

HECLA MINING
interval - 5,000 shares

Jan. 2, 1969
Feb. 3, 1969
Mar. 3, 1969
Apr. 1, 1969
May 1, 1969
June 2, 1969

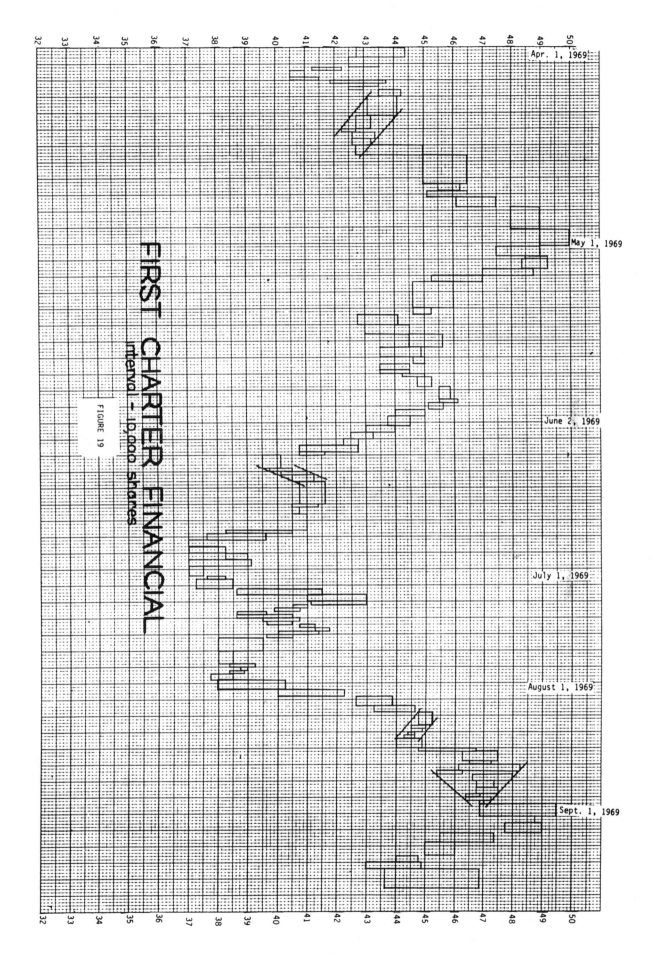

FIRST CHARTER FINANCIAL
Interval – 10,000 shares

FIGURE 19

CONSOLIDATION FORMATIONS

The analyst should always be looking for consolidation formations. These are the groundwork for his eventual commitments. He should not go into the stock when it is still in the consolidation formation but he should always be watching a group of consolidation formations, waiting for the signal to move. Let us state once again, for emphasis, never go into a stock when it appears to be through going down, and never short a stock because it seems to be through going up. Go into a stock early when it has finsihed going sideways, and has shown that it is embarking upon a new move.

In addition, do not try to go into a stock when it comes out of a flag or pennant. You should have been in the stock when the move began. It is now at least 1/3 over and probably much more profit than that has already gotten away. Look for a major consolidation area in some other stock.

CHAPTER VII

SUPPORT AND RESISTANCE

"If that stock ever gets back to what I paid for it, I'm bailing out!" How

many times have you said this, or heard other people say it? This is one of the emo-

tional responses which help to form resistance areas in stocks. Another comment is

"Next time it gets down there I'm darned sure going to buy it!" This emotion helps

to set support areas in stocks. It is coupled with: "If it gets back up there I'll give

them the stock."

In other words, the price of a stock is largely controlled by emotional re-

sponses, and people set up certain price levels in their minds, at which they are will-

ing to buy or sell a particular stock. As a consequence, stocks tend to establish price

levels at which they are likely to change direction. These levels are often obvious

and easily interpreted on charts, especially Equivolume charts. In this chapter we

will look at the way in which support and resistance manifest themselves, and how

they can be used to our trading advantage.

The Interchangeability of Support and Resistance. One of the most important

factors to be remembered when dealing with support and resistance, is that they can

replace one another. An area of support in a stock as it trades sideways becomes a resistance area once the level has been penetrated. Similarly, an area which continually stops upward moves will then become an area which stops downward moves once the stock has moved above the area.

The way in which support and resistance can occur at the same levels can be seen in Alcan Aluminium in Figure 20. The 28 1/2 area, the 30 area and the 31 1/2 area all act as both support and resistance areas. In addition, the 26-27 area acted various times as a support, but was not penetrated on this chart, and therefore was never called upon to act as a resistance area.

In this discussion the reader should realize that we are discussing only support and resistance levels. That is, we are not looking at the type of support that comes in at consistently higher or consistently lower prices. This type of price action will be covered in the next chapter, dealing with trend lines. What we are interested with here is the apparent fixation of a stock upon certain price levels. These levels are usually peculiar to each stock, but there are some levels which are so common that they tend to become support and resistance areas in many stocks. These are the round numbers, such as ten, twenty or fifty. The reason these numbers occur is also based upon emotions. People tend to decide "that stock will be a great buy if it ever gets down to twenty," or "when that stock gets to fifty, I'm getting out!" The prices in themselves mean nothing, but they are nice round numbers that are easily remembered.

Another area which can be depended upon to be a resistance area is a historic high. The fact that the stock turned back at 73 in 1948 should have very little

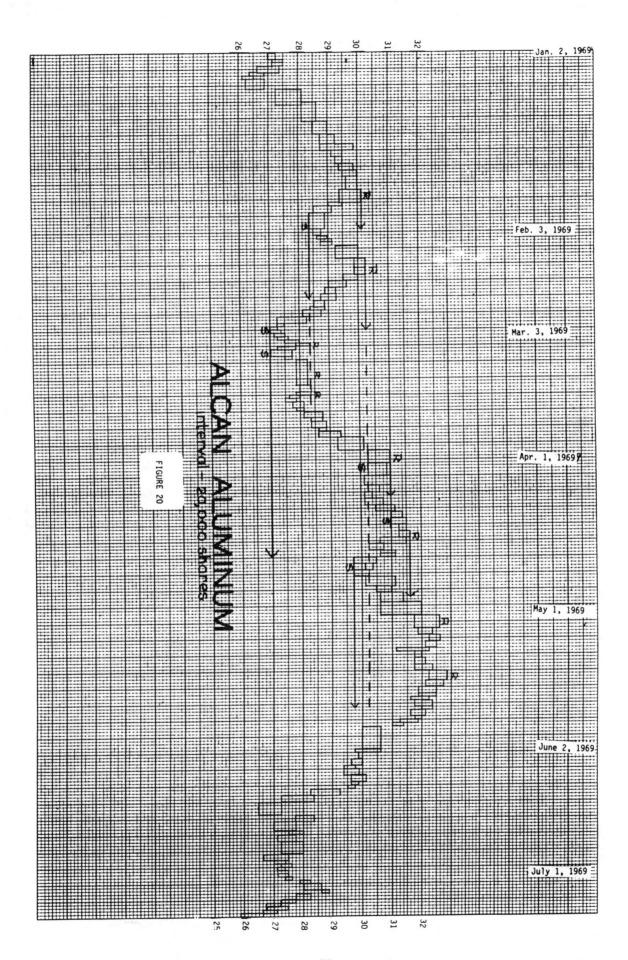

FIGURE 20

ALCAN ALUMINUM
Interval—20,000 Shares

bearing upon the stock in today's market. Actually, however, it will affect today's trading because people remember that old level and are watching it, perhaps wanting to sell at the all-time high. Similarly, historic lows will very often act as support areas. There are evidently buyers who recall the old lows, and have vowed to buy the stock if it ever gets back there.

Penetration of Support Levels. Equivolume charting makes it possible for us to take a close look at the penetration of levels. After a stock has established a support level it may return to it many times. The problem is that the stock will form an unprecise level. We can't be sure that the stock is going lower just because it moves an eighth through the previous low. The exact level is just not that reliable. What will tell us whether the penetration is significant is the range and the volume on the penetration.

If an old area of support is decisively penetrated and the volume increases, the stock has turned weak. If, in addition, the range increases, the signal is very reliable. The stock is evidently headed lower. A penetration, which shows an increase in the volume, but no widening of the spread, or a narrowing of the spread will tend to make the day "go square." This is likely to be a false move. In other words, the analyst should look for ease of movement. When a stock forms long narrow days it is moving easily. It is not encountering resistance. This is the type of movement which signals the successful penetration of an old area of support. Sometimes a stock will make a valid penetration with no increase in volume. Especially here, however, the range must get larger.

Penetration of Resistance Levels. When a stock has been constantly meeting upside resistance at a certain level, its penetration of that level follows the same rules as the downside penetrations of support outlined in the previous section. The main difference, however, is the volume. A good upward move necessitates volume to get it going. Stocks can drop of their own weight, in the absence of bidders, but they have to be pushed up by aggressive buying. For this reason an upward move, if it is to amount to anything must begin on volume. Therefore, an increase of volume is a requirement before buying a stock which is penetrating resistance. The buyer should beware of square days, just as he was on the downside breakouts, but he should be watching for a volume increase. The best indication is a rectangular day, but on heavier volume. If this is to occur, then the spread must be wider, indicating an ease in movement.

Figure 21 illustrates various resistance areas and their penetration. In this chart of Occidental Petroleum we see the stock set up an area at about 42 which first serves as a support area, is penetrated and serves as a resistance area, is later penetrated on the upside and serves again as a support area, and is finally penetrated again on the way down. We have numbered each of these penetrations. The downside move at point (1) is very obvious. Not only is the level decisively penetrated, but it is done on much heavier volume. The day is six columns wide, which represents more than 375,000 shares in this stock. Later this stock makes several attempts to get back through the area and accomplishes it at point (2). On this move the volume does not increase appreciably, but the spread is wider, giving the move validity.

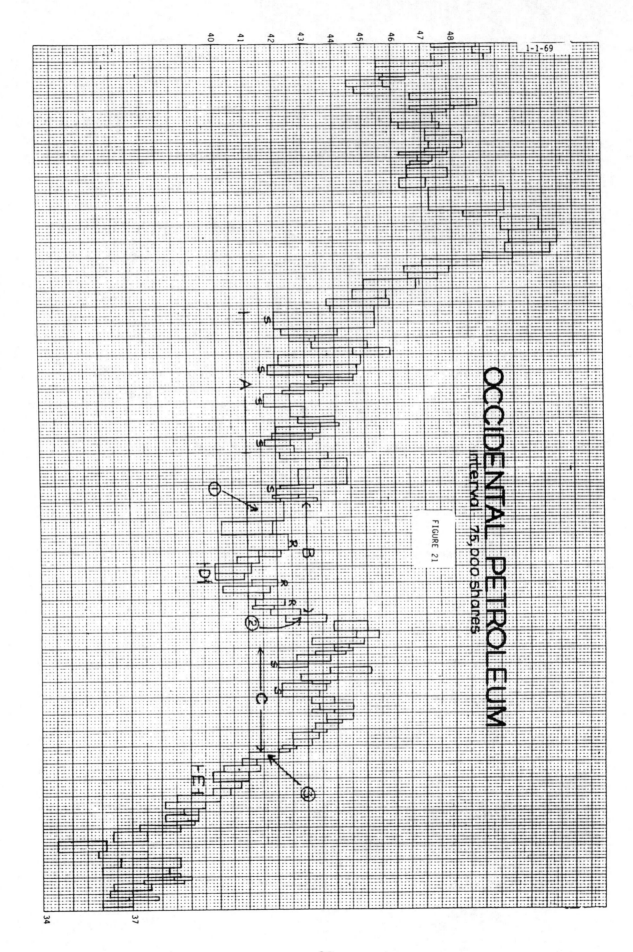

OCCIDENTAL PETROLEUM
Interval: 75,000 shares

FIGURE 21

1-1-69

After this the area of previous resistance once again becomes a support area, as the stock tries to move down through it. The penetration is accomplished at point (3), and the increase in volume coupled with a widening spread makes the breakout obvious. The validity of the move is finally confirmed when the stock hesitates at the 39 3/4 level and then penetrates the old lows with a widening spread. The stock is obviously headed lower.

Volume Relationships. When a stock forms a resistance area and then finally penetrates it, as in the previous example, a very significant relationship reveals itself. It must use up all of the old volume before it is able to complete the penetration. It is as though the people who bought stock on the lows must get a chance to get out of the stock again when these lows become trading highs before the stock is able to move back up. Whether this is true or not, the relationship exists.

Let us look again at the previous example of Occidental Petroleum. The original support area, which we have marked area "A" is almost the same size, measured horizontally as areas "B" and "C." A certain amount of volume had to be dissipated before the stock was prepared to penetrate the price level which was holding it back. On the other hand, area "D" was formed on fairly small volume, and was penetrated fairly easily after the hesitation at area "E."

The rule we arrive at is that volume leads to volume. If a chart area becomes a resistance level on heavy volume it will take heavy volume to penetrate it. If it was formed on light volume, only light volume will be necessary for the penetration. Accurate measurements are not possible, but a general cognizance of the previous volume will help the investor to know when a move is imminent. He should remember that the volume is the important factor, not the number of trading days. The stock could be at the resistance levels for many days but trade at light volume, and not be prepared for a penetration, or it could trade heavily enough to be ready to penetrate after only one or two sessions. Again, volume, not time, is the key to market action.

Support and resistance areas are very important to the trader. He should, in fact, be constantly watching for them. A good method is to put a small "R" on your chart above areas that appear to be presenting resistance to stock moves, and a small "S" below support areas. In addition, it is worthwhile to extend an arrow or line across the chart from these notations so that they can be later recognized when the stock again approaches these levels.

Trading Techniques. When a stock decisively penetrates an area of support or resistance it has provided the speculator a very reliable trading opportunity. Stocks tend to move between areas of support or resistance fairly rapidly, and a good penetration is rarely a false move. In addition, old areas of support or resistance make it fairly easy to ascertain where the move is headed.

The use of these areas makes stop orders especially worthwhile. In this case we are not talking about stops that are used to protect a profit or prevent a large loss; we are talking about the use of stop orders to establish a position. The speculator who sees a support level in a stock may feel that he does not want to sell the stock short unless it actually penetrates the support area decisively. Consequently he will place a "stop sell" order just below the old support area. If the stock breaks through the support and hits his price, he sells at the market, and is quickly in on the expected down move. Similarly, the investor or speculator who recognizes an area of resistance in a stock may place a stop order to buy the stock just above the resistance. If the stock breaks through the resistance he buys the stock at the best price then possible, and has probably caught the beginning of a move.

The speculator who is closely following the market probably does not need to use stop orders. He can recognize the moves when they occur, and act upon them. He will have the added advantage of being able to see the nature of the breakout. Is the volume heavier? Is the spread wider? In addition, he will be able to use the volume relationship we discussed earlier in order to anticipate when the move is likely to occur, and not have his money idle while he is waiting.

CHAPTER VIII

TREND LINES AND CHANNELS

To this point our primary consideration has been the study of stocks in equilibrium. At tops, bottoms, and consolidation areas stocks are within well defined boundaries of supply and demand. If the stock moves up it encounters a resistance to the move which we call supply. If it moves downward, it again moves into an area of opposition which we call demand. Between these two limits somewhat of an equilibrium exists. We have, to this point, assumed that the levels at which the supply and demand come in are constant. To an extent this is true, as we have seen in the chapter dealing with support and resistance. There are times, however, when supply and demand are changing values rather than absolutes. When this occurs we have trends.

A factor which is obvious to anyone who has so much as glanced at vertical line charts is the tendency for stocks to form well defined trends. Although a stock is advancing, it has minor fluctuations which tend to fit within a narrow upward channel. Over and over it will conform exactly to the limits of this channel, showing an uncanny regularity. In fact, the channel can often be recognized as a part of another long term channel, in which this upward move is only one small part. This tendency not only is just as obvious on Equivolume charts, it is even more reliable. Channels are amazingly well formed and adhered to by stocks when this method of charting is used.

When a stock is trading in a well defined trend, what is actually taking place is an adjustment in the stock price over a period of time. If the stock is in an uptrend, then there is no long term equilibrium in the stock. As we have said in the second chapter, each stock trade represents a temporary equilibrium, but nevertheless when a stock is moving up, there is a tendency for orders coming into the market to be buy orders rather than sell orders. Therefore, although a short term balance exists, a long-er term imbalance is affecting the stock.

The imbalance between longer term buying and selling causes each advance in the stock to be higher than its predecessor, and each decline to be shallower. There is a reluctance for new sellers to come in unless they can get a better price, and buy-ers are willing to pay somewhat higher prices on each rally. Since the same force which is causing the sellers to ask more is also causing the buyers to be willing to pay more, the changes in both groups should be approximately identical, thereby bringing about a parallel effect to the tops of the rallies and the bottoms of the declines. The stronger the factors causing the advance, the sharper the advance.

Vertical line charts assume that the change is based upon time, and that the stock will obey trend lines which represent a time constant on the horizontal axis. In reality, the stock has no concept of time, and time is not a direct determinant of the trend. What is important is that stock is changing hands, and changing the supply and demand picture in the stock. The more stock which is traded, the more change in the supply and demand equation. It happens that trend lines usually work well on vertical line charts because there is usually about the same amount of stock traded day after day in a particular company. Where trend lines are the least useful on vertical line charts is in very volatile issues. The vertical line chart is unable to compensate for the additional stock which changes hand on a day when the stock trades especially heavily. Equivolume charts give more emphasis to heavy volume days, and less emphasis to light volume days, thereby keeping the stock within its trend much better.

When a stock penetrates its trend line on a vertical line chart, there is some question of the validity of the signal. The signal on an Equivolume chart is more reliable. The reason is simply that the penetration could not have been due to volatility which was not compensated for.

Drawing Trend Lines. As obvious as it may sound, let us first emphasize that it takes two or more points to determine the location of a trend line. There is a tendency among chartists to try to put in lines before they are defined by the stock. It is only after the stock has reached two or more short term reversals that a trend line can be connected across them. This line can only be drawn across tops during a declining phase, and across bottoms during an advancing phase. To try to connect the bottoms during a declining phase, and thereby determine where support should be, is erroneous.

The chartist should be constantly experimenting with trend lines on his stocks. Some will hold true, and others be quickly invalidated. In this way, however, he will soon recognize the significant trends. After a trend is firmly established it is possible to look for a parallel line which will place the action of the stock within a channel. The second line, the one which is across the bottoms of a decline, or the tops in an advance, is called the return line. It is a guideline only. The stock is not required to stay within it. The main values to a return line are (1) it confirms the validity to the trendline, and (2) it gives you a good indication of a place to take short term profits. The return line in a downtrend will never be used as a buy indication, since it is foolish to buy a stock which is in an obvious downtrend. Similarly, the return line in an uptrend can never be used as a place to short the stock, but it might be used to take short term profits on long positions established earlier near the trendline.

Figure 22 shows the way in which a stock will form very reliable trends. In this case we see that Polaroid formed a variety of different trends, haveing little relation to one another, but all well bounded. We have shown the trend lines as solid lines, while the return lines, where they exist, are dotted.

Proponents of vertical line charts often draw in double trend lines which parallel one another. This is unnecessary on Equivolume charts. The double trend lines are used on volatile stocks, and are a result of fluctuations which the vertical line charts cannot compensate for.

Penetration of Trend Lines. Unlike the other penetrations we have studied, there is little that is distinctive about the penetration of a trendline. More often than not it is done with little change in either volume or spread. The day is likely

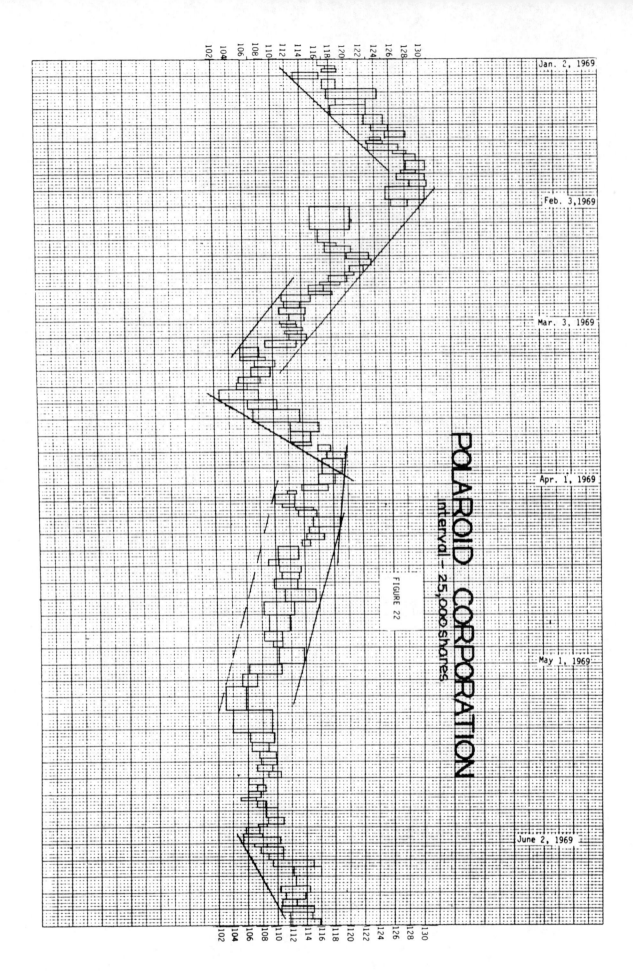

POLAROID CORPORATION
Interval – 25,000 shares

FIGURE 22

Jan. 2, 1969

Feb. 3, 1969

Mar. 3, 1969

Apr. 1, 1969

May 1, 1969

June 2, 1969

to look like any other day on the chart. The distinctive trading will not occur until the stock gets to a support or resistance area which it must penetrate. What we must look for is the penetration itself, and not a volume or spread indication. If the penetration is after an extended move we will already have had other clues at the termination of the move, and the penetration of the trendline only confirms our conclusions.

The one major exception to the above statements will be dealt with in the next chapter. When a stock penetrates a major trend line, and does it on a gap, then the spread and volume are special considerations.

It is too bad that there is no distinguishing characteristic about the penetration. It does not wave a red flag, making you recognize it as a turnaround. This does not make it unimportant, however. The penetration of a trendline on an Equivolume chart is very reliable. You probably have had a previous warning of what is happening, but if not, do not ignore the change in trend. If you own a stock which has been moving up, and it then goes sideways enough to penetrate the trend line, get out! It has told you that the advance is at least temporarily over, and the best you can now expect is a sideways move. You may later get another indication to get back in, but in the meantime you have avoided being locked into a sideways move, and you are not running the risk of a decline.

Figure 23 illustrates the penetration of trend lines in Phillips Petroleum. The early March upward move which penetrated the descending trendline was done on increasing volume with a narrowing of the spread, which made it especially con-

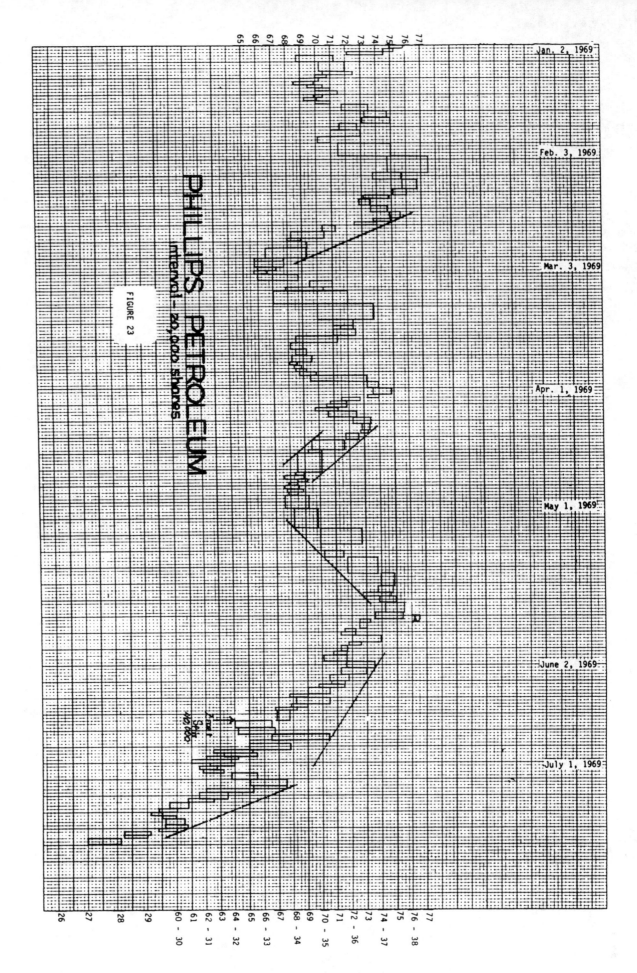

FIGURE 23

PHILLIPS PETROLEUM
interval—20,000 shares

Jan. 2, 1969

Feb. 3, 1969

Mar. 3, 1969

Apr. 1, 1969

May 1, 1969

June 2, 1969

July 1, 1969

vincing. After a rally which was terminated with plenty of warning (by returning twice to the tops, each time going more square) the stock again declined in a well defined channel. This was terminated by a penetration of the descending trendline in late April, again with heavier volume and a wider trading range. It had indicated the termination of the downward move. The next advance which lasted until mid-May ended by again going square. The top might have been hard to recognize, but the move through the ascending trendline signaled the end of the advance. As often happens, there was no great change in either trading range or volume to indicate that the penetration of the trendline was significant.

The reader will note on this chart the adjustment for a two for one split in June. The interval was therefore adjusted to 40,000 instead of 20,000 and the vertical scale doubled.

Finally, Phillips goes into a long term downtrend which continues off the bottom of this chart. A beginning trendline was drawn which connected the first three tops. Later the decline became steeper, and a new trendline seemed more appropriate. In a long advance or decline, various trendlines, becoming steeper and steeper often occur. The last trendline should be the one used to determine penetration, if it is obviously a well established trend. If the steepest trendline is penetrated, it is tempting to look at the earlier less steep trendlines, and hope that the stock will hold at those levels. This comes under the category of "kidding yourself" and should be avoided. When a well established trendline is penetrated, believe it.

High Volume Move Terminations. When a stock has been in a steep upward

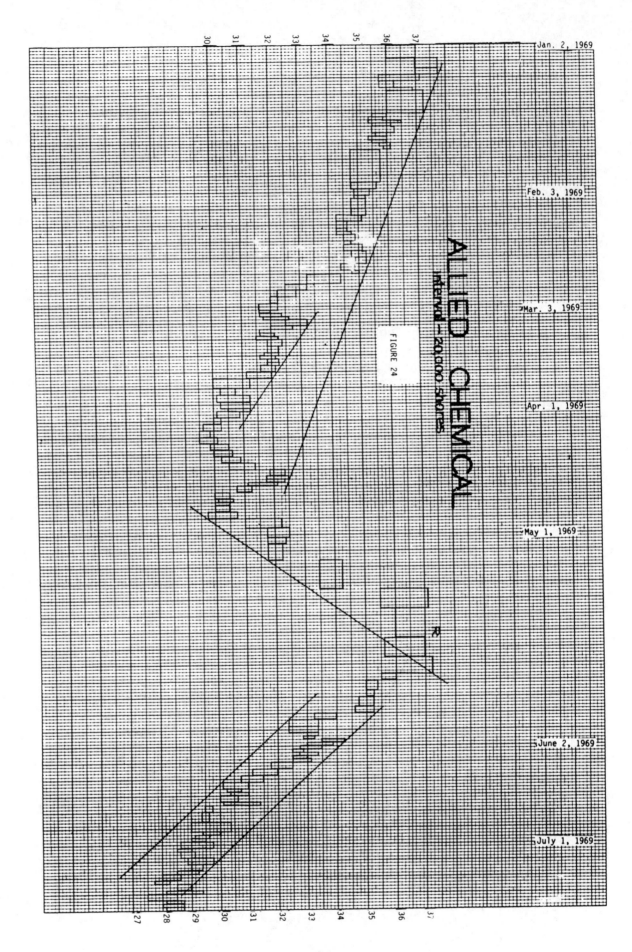

ALLIED CHEMICAL
interval—20,000 shares

FIGURE 24

or downward move it is usually terminated by a "blowoff" in which volume gets very heavy. Equivolume charts are especially helpful when this happens. A look at Figure 24 will illustrate why. The mid-April to mid-May move was ended in just this way. Because the Equivolume chart moves the entire pattern sideways on any heavy volume trading the ascending trendline was penetrated while the top was still forming. A vertical line chart would have appeared to still be maintaining the upward trend until a week later when the stock was two points lower.

Trend lines provide the chartist with a very reliable set of indicators of market action. They are easy to see and draw in. The primary problem is that many different trend lines can be drawn depending upon the points used. The best answer to this is be logical. Stand back from the chart and notice the overall move. It should then be possible to see the way in which the prices are trending, and draw in logical trend lines. Since the location of trend lines is subjective, the results from following them are only as good as the skill of the chartist in establishing their location. Using them correctly, and believing what they say, can add to your profits.

CHAPTER IX

GAPS

In any stock there are times when circumstances will cause it to form a gap. That is, there will exist an area in which no trading occurred between two days of market activity. In the time that the market was closed, and no stock changed hands, some factor or combination of factors upset the supply and demand equation in the stock, so that it traded during the next day in a different price area, never overlapping the previous day's trading range.

For the most part, we need not be concerned with the reason for the gap. The fact that it exists tells us that something is happening in the stock. As technical analysts, we need to know that there has been a change in the supply and demand equation which has pushed the stock into a new trading area, but there is no reason to search for the factors which have caused this change. They may be factors which are known throughout the marketplace, or may be known only to a few insiders, but in either case this should not affect our judgment. The market, through its own action, will tell the entire story.

The only exceptions to the above are the ex-dividend gap, and the small gaps that occur in inactive stocks. In either case, the gaps became obvious through their insignificance. The fact that they are not accompanied by anomalies in volume generally will show them for what they are.

When a stock sells ex-dividend the price of the stock will usually reflect that dividend. The buyers of the stock are no longer participants in the forthcoming dividend, and are therefore likely to be willing to pay that much less for the stock.

As we have previously said, these gaps are usually easily recognized and provide no problem for the analyst. However, he should still make sure of the nature of a gap, and see if it is caused by going ex-dividend. If, for example, a stock was ex a 10 percent stock dividend, it would cause a major price change in the stock, which would be misleading if not attributed to the dividend. Especially so, since the payment of a large stock dividend is often accompanied by heavier trading, due to an increase in the float. In fact, we have seen in previous sections that we adjust our charts for a large increase in the float, by reducing the sensitivity of the volume scale when a split occurs.

Some stock are very inactive, and are therefore especially prone to form gaps. Such a stock is easy to recognize. It will form gaps quite often, and yet continue within its trading range. In addition, there will be little variation in volume accompanying the gaps. They will, in other words, be merely a part of the normal trading.

All gaps that do not fit into one of the two above exceptions should be scrutinized by the analyst. They provide a very obvious and interpretable indication of a change in investor sentiment regarding a stock. Properly used they will help to point out the beginnings of new moves, the continuation of a move, or the termination of a move. They should be considered one of the analyst's most valuable tools.

Let us not forget that a gap represents a period when there was no trading in the stock. A vertical line chart and even more so a point and figure chart tend to merge days together, and consider trading as a stream rather than a series of disconnected events. In Equivolume charting each day becomes a separate analysis of a supply-demand equilibrium. The gap, regardless of its size, represents no balancing of supply and demand. The balance is only reached during the ensuing trading period. Consequently, the analyst using Equivolume charts should not be swayed by considering the extent of the gap, but should study the trading periods which embrace the gap.

Necessary Information. When a gap occurs, there are certain things the analyst must know in order to interpret it. He must ask himself certain questions in order to properly categorize the gap, and therefore to use it for predicting the market action which is likely to occur afterwards.

The trading prior to the gap is as important as the gap, and the way in which it occurs. The analyst should look for three pieces of information about the trading prior to a gap. First, is the direction of the stock and its position in that move. Has the stock been in a sideways move for some time, or has it recently been moving upward or downward. We do not mean that he should try to ascertain the long term direction of the stock. It is necessary, however, to notice what the stock has done during the last few days or weeks. In other words, is the stock in a minor uptrend, a sideways move or a minor downtrend? Also he should note whether this is part of an extended move, and whether it appears to be a move that has just started or one that is likely to have run its course.

Secondly, the analyst should ask himself what sort of volume has been involved in the recent trading. He must know whether the gap involves unusual volume, or is in keeping with the normal trading in this stock. He should especially note any unusual days in the few days preceding the gap, such as square days or very thin rectangles.

The third information necessary about the trading prior to the gap involves the day immediately preceding the gap, or rather, the first of the two days which embrace the gap. He should note whether the day was in the normal pattern of trading, or whether traders already knew something and were starting to react to whatever factors were to later form the gap. Was it a day of heavier than usual trading, and if so, did the stock run into either massive supply or massive demand causing it to form a square or oversquare day. If this was the case, then it should be possible to see which factor caused it to go square, and whether it was overcoming a resistance in forming a gap, or moving away from that resistance.

Having ascertained the answers to the above questions, the analyst is ready to look at the gap, and the day which follows the gap and forms it. Again, the most important two pieces of information will be the volume and the range of trading on the after gap day. This will show itself as either a thin day or a square or oversquare day. In addition, it is necessary to observe the comparative volume. Is trading heavier than normal? Usually a small gap with no appreciable change in volume has little or no significance. The size of the gap is also an indication of the strength of the move, and should therefore be noted, but it should not receive undue emphasis. In order to properly analyze the situation, we must look at the supply and demand picture which unfolds as trading occurs. The gap represents a change in investor sentiment which took place while the market was closed. No volume occurred during that time, so it does not directly affect our analysis.

Gaps Out of a Sideways Area. The most obvious, and very often the most valuable gaps are those that develop after a sideways move in a stock. They are easily noticed and recognized because they usually follow a period of fairly low volume and quite uniform days. This sort of gap is strongly signaling a change in character in the stock. Something has happened which has brought about a reappraisal of the stock. Speculators have stepped in, and are moving it on heavier trading. This is the sort of move which is usually termed a "breakout."

Such a move is seen in the gap which occurred in National General in the accompanying Figure 25. Between mid-March and the end of April the stock had moved in a fairly narrow trading range, and most days had involved minimum volume and a small trading range. Then on April 30th the stock moved ahead on heavier volume, and left a gap, which separated it from the prior trading range. As can be seen, this was the forerunner of a substantial move for the stock. The breakaway day did not involve a spectacular increase in volume, and the trading range was not unusual, but it was a better day than had been seen recently in the stock, and showed a change of character in the trading. An additional sign of strength is seen in the

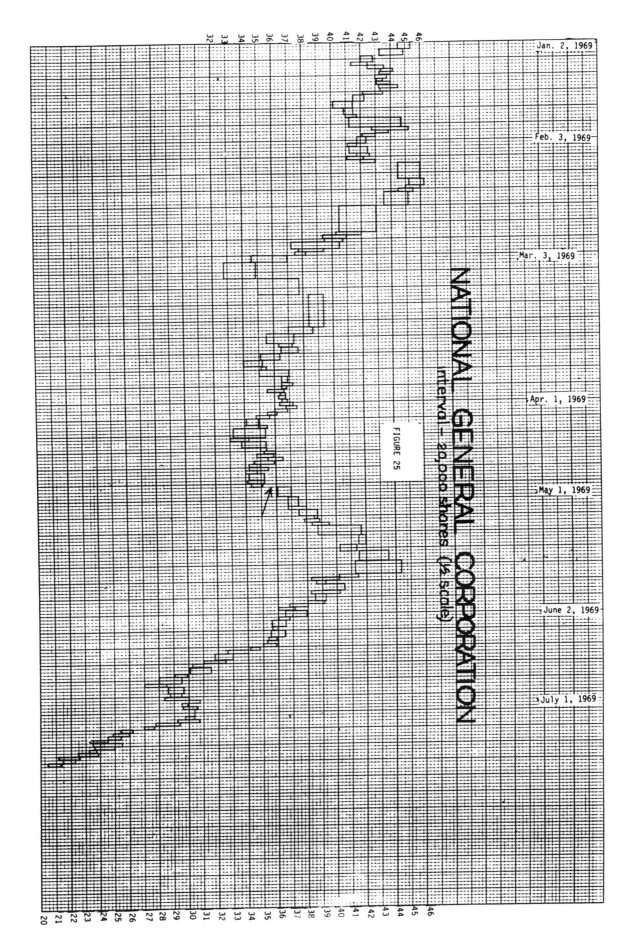

NATIONAL GENERAL CORPORATION

Interval = 20,000 shares (½ scale)

FIGURE 25

Jan. 2, 1969

Feb. 3, 1969

Mar. 3, 1969

Apr. 1, 1969

May 1, 1969

June 2, 1969

July 1, 1969

fact that the descending trendline through the March and April highs is breached by the gap.

A similar move, this time on the downside, can be seen in American Telephone in early June of 1969, in Figure 9 in Chapter 4. American Telephone is such a widely held and actively traded stock that wide variations in volume are not common, nor are gaps. In this case, there was little change in volume, but the gap certainly signaled a change in character for the stock. The top that had been forming in the last month had found its lows over and over again just below the 56 area. The gap decisively penetrated this and destroyed what hopes might have remained that the stock would resume its advance. Neither the volume nor the trading range were unusual in this case, but the gap made obvious the fact that something had changed.

A gap out of a trading area need not penetrate the resistance or support areas which have been confining the stock in order to be significant. Usually, however, this occurs also, and becomes a further indication as to the future direction of the stock. The factor that is necessary, however, is an increase in volume. This will, of course, be shown as a wider day, but may be a rectangular day or a square or over-square day.

The typical gap out of a sideways area, whether a base or a top, will show a doubling or tripling of normal volume, and a wider trading range than has been observed in recent trading. Whether the day is rectangular or square will indicate the amount of resistance opposing the trading after the gap and show the probable near term market action.

For example, a stock gaps upward out of a trading range, and penetrates its old highs with a marked increase in volume. The trading range is narrow enough, however, so that the increased volume makes it an oversquare day. This action would indicate that the stock has definitely changed its trading pattern, and appears to be embarking upon a substantial advance. The oversquare day, however, indicates that there should be a pullback prior to much more appreciation. The pullback can be expected to take the price back to the old tops, or even slightly through them. The observant trader will wait for the pullback before buying. The pullback should, of course, be on lower volume than that which accompanied the breakout gap. High volume would serve as a warning to hold off on buying.

Similarly, if the stock had gapped up but the day had been rectangular, rather than square, it would show little overhead supply, and would be a signal to buy immediately, and not wait for a pullback. The stock is acting so strong, and moving so easily that the pullback probably will not occur.

Reversal Gaps. Closely related to the gaps described in the previous section are gaps that go contrary to a trend, after the trend is well established. While the previous gaps signaled a change from a sideways move to an upward or downward move, these gaps signal a change from an upward or downward trend to a sideways move.

It is natural for us to think that when a stock is through going down it will go up, but this is not usually the case. After a long period when supply has been pushing the stock downward, there will usually be a substantial period when supply and demand are in a balance, and prices trend sideways in a narrow trading range. It is later that demand becomes stronger, and prices begin to advance. Admittedly, there are instances where a stock will quickly change directions, and start a new advance with little or no base building, but even then Equivolume charting will almost always show a fairly wide base due to the heavier volume which accompanies such a bottom.

For our purposes it is best to watch for the change which turns a down move into a sideways move, recognize the sideways move, and then watch for an indication of the beginning of an upward move. Even if the bottoming is brief, both signals will occur. Buying at the end of the downward move carries two dangers. One is that the base will be long, and money will be doing nothing for quite a period of time. The other is the danger that the signal that the down move had ended only meant "for the time being." After a sideways move, the stock could break out in either direction, perhaps leading to a loss, if the breakout is on the downside.

A reversal gap indicates the end, at least temporarily of a well established trend. It can be a down gap in a stock which has been advancing, or an upward gap in a stock which has been declining. It will always be accompanied by heavier volume if it is significant, and it is usually accompanied by a larger trading range. After such a gap, there may be some continuation to the move, but a pullback to or close to the old levels is to be expected. This is a part of the base or top building. Again, the nature of the gap day will indicate the extent to which the move is likely to carry. A square or oversquare day indicates an almost immediate return to the old tops or lows while a rectangular day shows that the move probably has further to go.

This signal is very often accompanied by other factors which are in themselves significant. Very often a reversal gap will also bridge the descending trendline in a down move or the ascending trendline in an up move. This gives further strength to the signal, but still can only be interpreted as a change to a sideways move. If, however, the gap also takes the stock above a previous resistance area, then there is a strong likelihood that a new move in the opposite direction has begun. We have, then, one trading day which gives two signals: first, a change from a decline to a sideways move, and secondly, a change from a sideways move to an advance.

Figure 26 of Pacific Petroleum contains a good illustration of a reversal gap. After a fast rise in May, the stock went square on June third. The following day a small gap was formed, but the trading was heavy, and indicated a reversal. In fact, the ascending trendline was penetrated, also. It was indicating the termination of the advance. When the stock reached 43 5/8 it had run into heavy overhead supply, which had caused the more square day. The next day the selling had become heavy enough so the stock gapped downward, and continued down, under heavy liquidation.

A similar gap, this time in a reversal from the bottom, is seen in Figure 27 of Collins Radio. The mid-March turn leaves no doubt that the stock has completed the decline and is starting up. In one day of trading it gapped up, penetrated its descending trendline, and then penetrated the resistance at 55 1/2.

Continuation Gaps. When a stock is already moving either upward or downward, there are often gaps which go in the same direction as the trend. These are

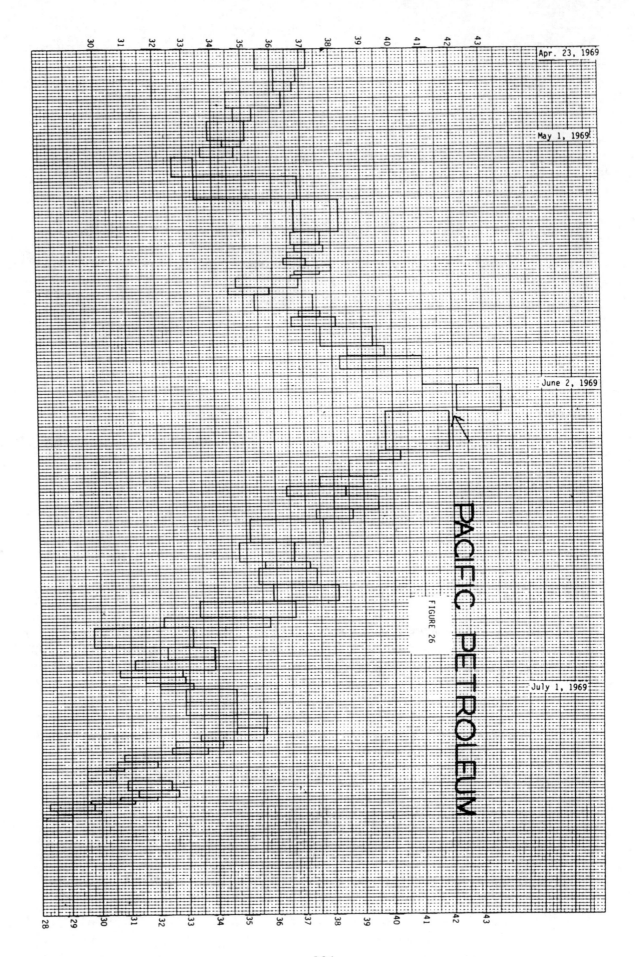

PACIFIC PETROLEUM

FIGURE 26

Apr. 23, 1969

May 1, 1969

June 2, 1969

July 1, 1969

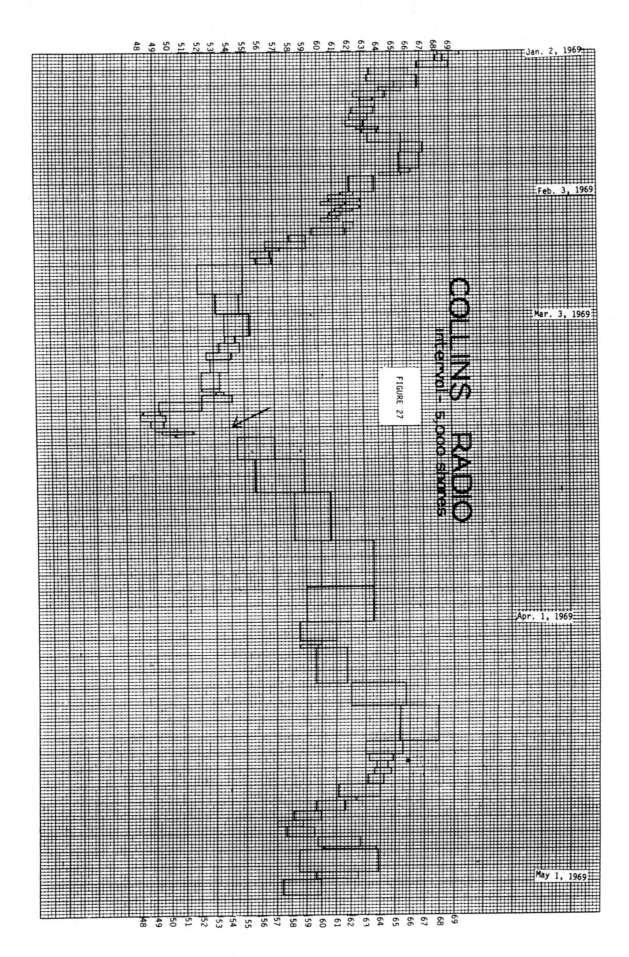

COLLINS RADIO
Interval- 5,000 shares

FIGURE 27

Jan. 2, 1969

Feb. 3, 1969

Mar. 3, 1969

Apr. 1, 1969

May 1, 1969

called continuation gaps. Three different types are common, and are each interpreted differently. They occur at different times in a move, and have their own volume and spread characteristics.

As a stock begins an upward move, for example, the sudden increase in buying pressure will cause it to gap upward. The volume is usually no heavier than the preceding day, but the spread is likely to be wider. The stock has broken away from its old trading area and is starting to run. The gap indicates the beginning of a move which is likely to be quite substantial. It shows that the buying pressure is very strong. The nature of the gap is recognized by the increase in spread, with or without an increase in volume. It very often accompanies a penetration of a resistance area.

As the move progresses, the stock will often gap upward again in what is known as a runaway gap. The stock is moving so fast that it opens higher than the previous day's highs. The gap is recognized as a runaway gap by the tall narrow days on both sides of it. The stock is running fast, with little resistance, so the days are narrow. The runaway gap tells us that the move has further to go. Very often they occur as the stock completes about 50% of its eventual move.

After the advance has run a long way the third type of gap is likely to occur. This is known as an exhaustion gap. It tells us that the move is completed. The exhaustion gap is characterized by a much more square day on the far side of the gap. After moving easily the stock has run into heavy supply. It is telling us that the advance is being halted and the stock should be sold.

Closely related to the exhaustion gap is the island reversal. In this case the stock gaps up and goes square, trades for some time above the gap, and then gaps back down through the same area, leaving an island of trading, separated from the rest of the chart by gaps. This is an excellent indication that the advance has finished. The first gap should have told us that the advance was over, the second gap told us that a decline was starting.

Looking again at Figure 27 we can see examples of all three types of continuation gaps in less than a month of trading. In late January there is a very obvious breakaway gap, with heavier volume. This is followed in mid-February by a runaway gap, and the move is completed in late February by an exhaustion gap.

Figure 28 of Studebaker-Worthington contains many gaps, which we have numbered consecutively. This is a stock with a tendency to gap often, but nevertheless, all of the gaps conform to the requirements we have set forth in this chapter. They are as follows:

1) A runaway gap. Wide spread, easy movement.

2) An exhaustion gap. Note the squareness of the next day.

3) A gap within the trading range. No increase in range or volume. This gap is meaningless.

4) Another trading range gap.

5) These gaps are all meaningless. The light volume indicates there is just light trading causing the gaps.

6) A breakaway gap. Note the increase in volume.

7) Another breakaway, this time going up.

8) Runaway gap. Wide spread and low volume after the gap.

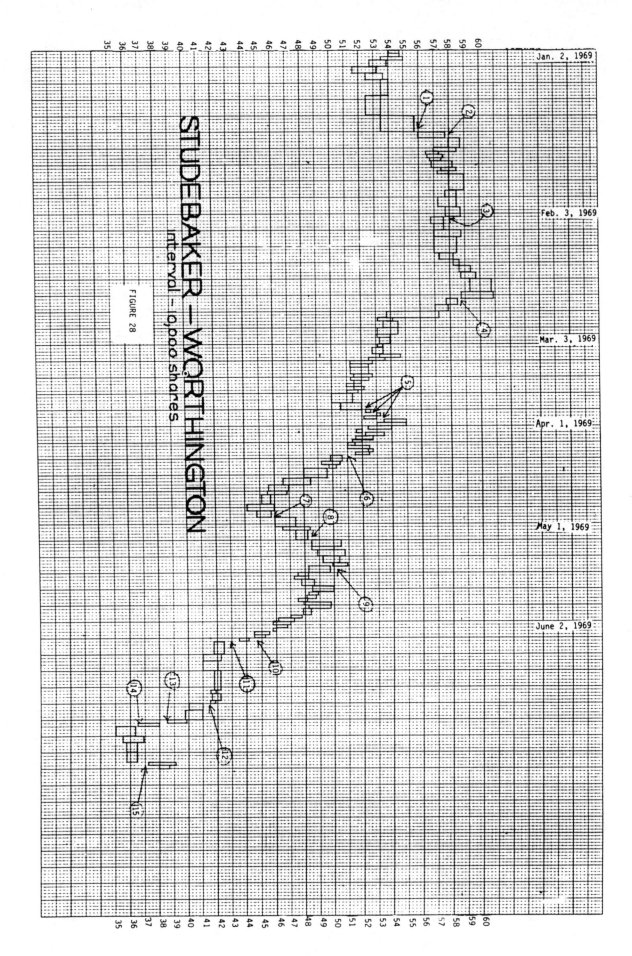

STUDEBAKER—WORTHINGTON

interval — 10,000 shares

FIGURE 28

9) A reversal gap. It penetrated the trendline, indicating an end to the advance.

10) Runaway gap.

11) Exhaustion gap. Note the square day.

12) Another breakaway, after the sideways move.

13) Runaway gap.

14) Exhaustion Gap. Increase in volume. Stock is meeting demand.

15) Another breakaway, which turns the previous four days into an Island Reversal.

CHAPTER X

TARGETS

The greatest value in point and figure charting is the establishment of price

objectives or "targets." In fact, we feel that this is the only worthwhile use for point

and figure charting. It has been found that Equivolume charts can also be used to es-

tablish targets, and thereby eliminate the need for keeping more than one chart for

a single secuity being studied. In fact, as we will show, the Equivolume method is

a direct reading, while point and figure arrives at its results in a more round about

way.

Let us first look at the point and figure method of price projection. The

theory is that a stock which is in a sideways move is either under accumulation or

distribution. As the traders start to work their way into or out of a stock they move

the price of the stock, and then back off from it, letting it return to its previous trad-

ing level. Each time that they do this the stock posts two new columns on the point

and figure chart. The more the accumulation or distribution, the more times it will

move back and forth, and consequently the wider the sideways move as illustrated on

the point and figure chart. When the traders have completed their accumulation or

distribution the stock is moved out of the trading range, and the mark-up or markdown stage begins. The extent of the move is directly related to the width of the sideways move. On a one-point chart the stock will advance just as many points as the number of columns which made up the sideways move. On a three-point chart the upward or downward move is expected to be three times the accumulation or distribution area. Figure 29 shows this type of price projection.

The immediate reaction is "Why should the stock move up just that many points?" The method is an artificial one, in that there seems to be little relationship between the extent of the sideways move and the number of points the stock moves. However, the fact remains that it does work. Point counts can be made which work out exactly over and over again. It makes it possible to estimate the anticipated profit upon entering a commitment.

We feel that it works for two reasons. First, the sideways move on a point and figure chart is an approximation of volume. If a stock is trading back and forth, and forming columns on the point and figure chart, stock is being traded. The more price action, the more volume. Secondly, advances in stocks, although sometimes more rapid than at other times, have an average slope of 45 degrees. In other words, the vertical dimension of the advance is just about equal to the horizontal distance during the advance.

Equivolume Price Projections. In Equivolume charting we are able to look directly at volume, rather than through the medium of price reversals in point and figure charts. This brings us to the realization that there is a direct cause and effect relationship in stocks. For a stock to have an appreciable move (the effect) we must

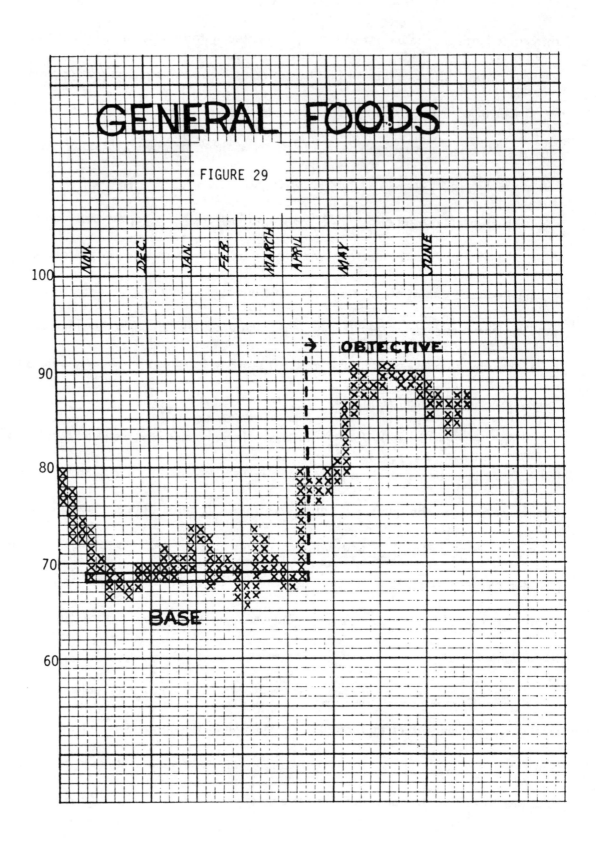

GENERAL FOODS

FIGURE 29

first have a sideways move that forms the foundation for it (the cause). If a stock

has had a minor sideways move it can only have a minor advance or decline before

starting a new sideways move.

Not only is the cause and effect relationship apparent, it is related directly

to volume. The cornerstone of price projection in Equivolume charting is: <u>volume</u>

<u>leads to volume.</u> The volume that is generated in the building of a base is almost ex-

actly the volume dissipated in the ensuing advance. Similarly, the volume occurring

in a top formation is very close to the same as the volume involved in the subsequent

decline. If this is accepted we can now see why point and figure counts work so often.

Since the price moves indicate an approximation of volume, and since the average

move on a point and figure chart follows a 45 degree slope, the upward move is like-

ly to be very nearly of the same extent as the width of the base.

<u>Using These Principles.</u> In order to profit from these ideas, it is necessary to

understand how to apply them. The main consideration is that a stock should have

formed a substantial base before we buy it. If the base is small, the move after the

breakout is also going to be small, unless the stock follows a very steep slope in its

advance. Of course, if the slope of the advance is very gradual, even a wide base

will not generate big profits. When the stock has completed a base, and then given

a buy indication, we have no way of knowing what the slope of the advance is going

to be, but can assume that it will probably be steep enough for a reasonable profit if

the base was quite wide. Only after two ascending bottoms have been formed can

we draw in a trendline, and get an idea of the rate of the rise. Then by measuring the width of the base and projecting the same distance again along the horizontal

axis we can see how much volume will be dissipated before the move is likely to run

out of steam. By projecting upward from this point to the trendline we get an indica-

tion of the probable extent of the move.

Figure 30 shows this type of price projection in Ford. There are two separate

advances shown on the chart, each with its causative base, bringing about an advance

which utilizes the available volume. Note that the first advance has a smaller base,

but generated bigger profits because the slope of the advance is so much steeper.

The first advance is steeper than a 45 degree slope, while the second advance is just

slightly less than 45 degrees. In both cases, however, the investor could see that

enough base had been formed to justify a profitable advance. There was no way of

knowing when the moves started how far they would go since the slope was not yet

established.

We have, so far, been talking about advances from a base. The same methods

apply equally well to declines from a top. Figure 31 shows such a move. The chart

actually contains many other intermediate moves that could also be noted for their

predictive value. Here, however, we have marked the major top and the subsequent

major decline. It can easily be seen that the volume across the top is equivalent to

the volume in the subsequent decline.

Accuracy. It should be pointed out that no method is foolproof. The way in

which moves can be predicted by this method is often uncanny, but at times it will

not work out exactly. In addition, the measuring of an accumulation or distribution

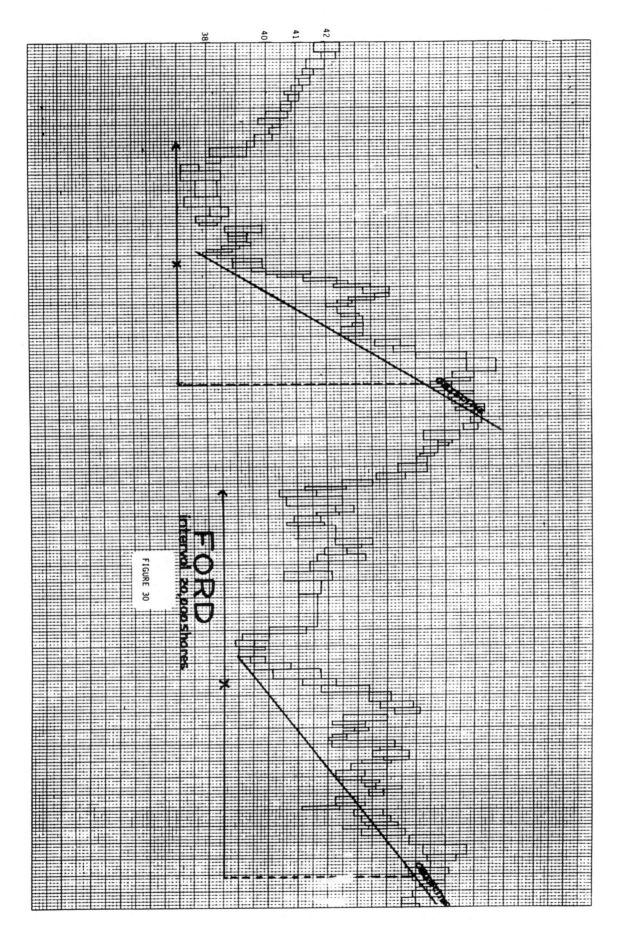

FORD
interval 20, 000 shares

FIGURE 30

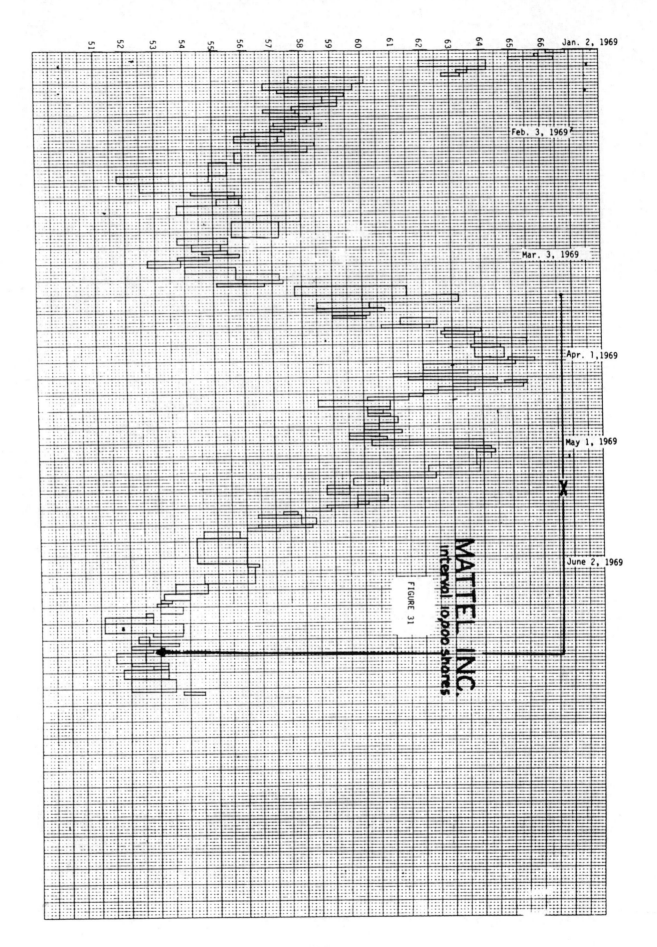

MATTEL, INC.
interval 10,000 shares

FIGURE 31

Jan. 2, 1969

Feb. 3, 1969

Mar. 3, 1969

Apr. 1, 1969

May 1, 1969

June 2, 1969

area is somewhat subjective.   Only with practice will the chartist be able to correct-

ly decide where the areas of accumulation or distribution begin and end. The price

projections arrived at should only serve as guidelines. They are less important than

the many principles put forth in the preceding chapters.   If the stock has advanced,

but has not yet used up all of the volume, and it then goes square and starts to de-

cline, the investor should take his profits or at least put a stop order in to protect

them, regardless of the anticipated and so far unfulfilled objective. In addition, the

volume projection should take precedence over the price projection. If the volume

has been used up, but the stock has not reached the price objective established by

the trendline, the stock should be sold.

CHAPTER XI

CHARTING THE AVERAGES

If Equivolume charting works so well on individual issues, why not apply the same principles in analyzing the entire market? It stands to reason that it should work, and in fact it does, but there are some special considerations.

Equivolume charting owes its value to variation in volume. Large swings in volume, of course, provide the signals we are looking for. The drawback to averages such as the Dow-Jones Industrials is just that; they are averages. Averaging smooths out individual anomalies. When you are dealing with a group of stocks the action of one is masked by the others. A stock which jumps upward on volume is only one of thirty stocks in the Dow, and its individual performance is reduced to one-thirtieth. In the same manner, volume figures reflect the entire market, or the entire volume on the stocks used in the averages. The individual moves and the volume anomalies are lost in the grouping.

Method of Construction. In order to somewhat reduce the above effect, and yet get a look at what the market is doing it is necessary to abandon one of the principles of Equivolume charting, that of constant volume along the "X" axis. It can be seen that a normal trading day in today's markets is in the neighborhood of 10,000,000 shares on the New York Stock Exchange. Using the same methods we have used for

individual issues we would multiply by .67 and come up with 6,700,000 shares as our

first breakpoint. This would mean that any volume of 6.7 million shares or under would

be charted one column wide. Any volume better than 6.7 million but up to 13.4

million would be two columns wide, and any volume over 13.4 million but up to 19.1

million would be three columns wide.

One can readily see the drawbacks to the above method. From July of 1968

through July of 1970, a period of two years, there would only have been two days on

which the volume was low enough to be plotted only one column wide. Almost all

trading days would be two columns wide, giving the chartist little to base his judg-

ment on. During the same time interval there were only eight trading sessions which

would extend to the fourth column on our chart, and no days which would qualify

for the fifth column.

In order to avoid this lack of sensitivity we have used a larger starting

breakpoint, and smaller intervals thereafter. It appears to work out best if the 8 mil-

lion level is used as the first point, and 4 million share intervals thereafter. The re-

sult is:

Up to 8 million shares	1 space
8 million to 12 million	2 spaces
12 million to 16 million	3 spaces
16 million to 20 million	4 spaces
20 million to 24 million	5 spaces

The reader should keep in mind that the above table fits very well for the

market at the time the book is being written. In ten years the market may be trading in far larger volumes. At that time perhaps this table would make a chart which was so wide as to be useless. The chartist must fit a scale to the market in which he is operating.

In constructing a chart of the averages the intraday highs and lows should be used, rather than the half hourly or hourly extremes. If the chart is to be accurate, it must show the true maximums and minimums, and therefore the actual trading range.

Analysis. Basically the same rules which are applied to individual issues apply to the analysis of the averages on an Equivolume chart. Just as in the stocks we have studied in the preceding sections, we are interested primarily in the ease or difficulty of movement. We will not see startling differences day to day, however, and must be more aware of slight differences as they occur. The averages may show that the market is running into resistance, in which case the volume is likely to stay high or increase while the spread narrows. There will never be any square or over-square days, however. The differences will be much more subtle. Conversely, even when the market is advancing or declining rapidly, the days won't look like the very tall and narrow days we are used to seeing in individual stocks.

Tops and Bottoms. Almost all turning points in the averages will appear on our charts as a rounded formation. There are few rapid and abrupt changes. This is even more true of tops than bottoms. Typically an intermediate term market top will be characterized by heavier volume days. They may individually be somewhat more square, but it is in their grouping that the distribution becomes apparent. A firm level forms which the averages are unable to penetrate, and heavy trading will occur in the vicinity of this level. Figures 32, 33 and 34 represent the Dow-Jones Industrial Averages from the beginning of 1967 to the middle of 1970. The top in February of 1969, and the later top in May of the same year show this type of topping. It is apparent in each case that the market has run into very strong resistance. The drop away from the resistance with an increase in the spread, and a penetration of the ascending trendline signals the inability of the market to penetrate the resistance.

The formation of a bottom is likely to be somewhat different. A sharper turn is likely, especially after a steep decline. Rather than square days the days are likely to encompass a wide range, but on heavy volume. Of course, as we have pointed out in previous sections, the levels at which the turn occurs are likely to be tested, usually on lower volume with a narrower spread. Such market action can be seen in February of 1970. After a series of relatively low volume days volume picked up appreciably, and the spread became wider. The turn was followed by two later tests of the same approximate area, each time with lighter volume and a narrower spread. This led later to a substantial advance in the market.

In dealing with tops and bottoms the analyst should be especially aware that days can be and often must be grouped in order to form a recognizable signal. The market is not a series of individual days, but a flowing pattern, in which the change from up to down may take some time to develop.

Trendlines. Especially important in working with charts of averages are trendlines. They are drawn just as they would be on an individual issue, with an ascending trendline under an advance and a descending trendline above a decline. The pene-

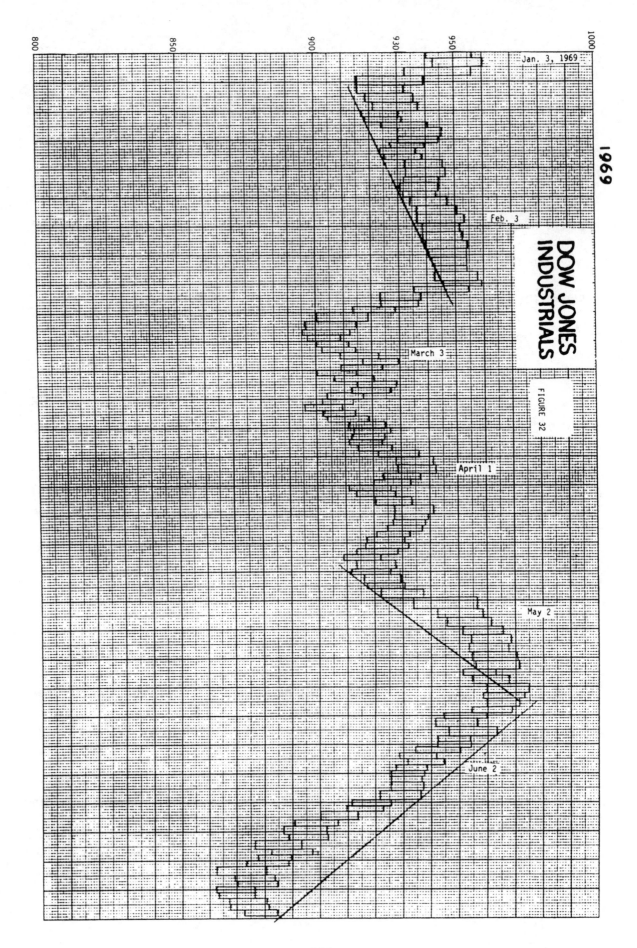

DOW JONES
INDUSTRIALS

FIGURE 32

1969

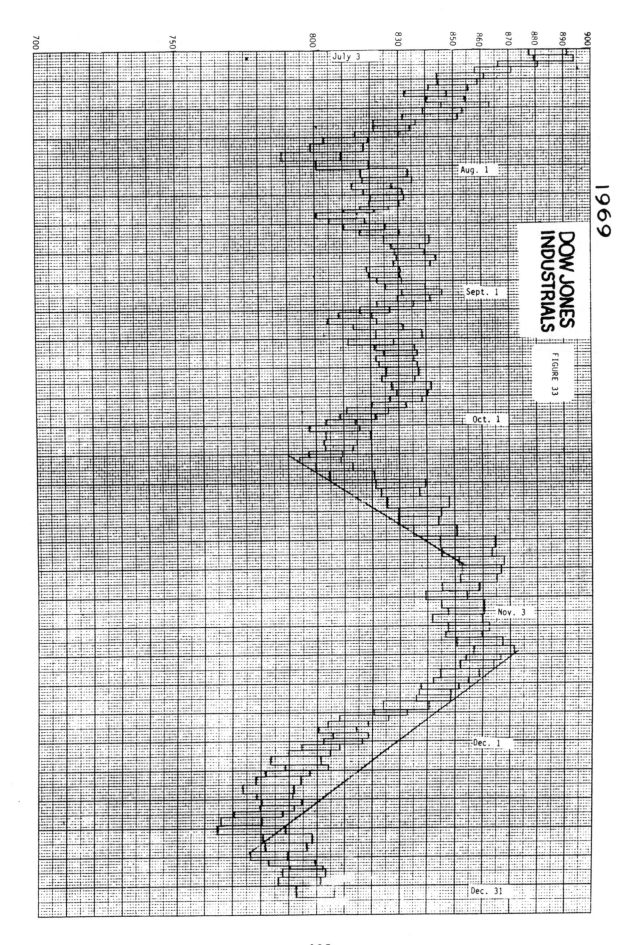

1969

DOW JONES
INDUSTRIALS

FIGURE 33

July 3

Aug. 1

Sept. 1

Oct. 1

Nov. 3

Dec. 1

Dec. 31

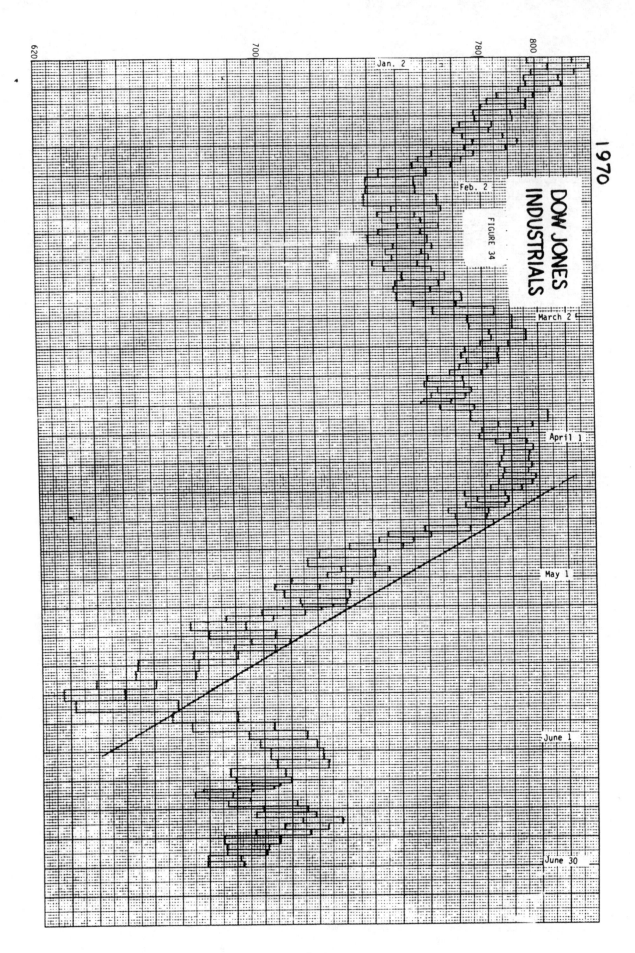

1970

DOW JONES
INDUSTRIALS

FIGURE 34

Jan. 2

Feb. 2

March 2

April 1

May 1

June 1

June 30

620

700

780

800

tration of these trendlines is usually very reliable. The reader will see various trendlines drawn on the accompanying charts, and can note how well they signaled each
change in direction.

Support and Resistance. Almost as important as trendlines are areas of support and resistance. As the market moves upward and downward it seems to have an
uncanny way of remembering old levels. If it turned upward from a support area once
months ago, it is very likely to do so again. In addition, as in individual issues, support areas tend to later become resistance areas and vice versa. It can be seen on
the accompanying charts how the December 1969 lows became the February 1970
highs. Likewise, the April 1969 highs were to establish a level which was later the
support level in May of the same year.

Price Objectives. The one preceding chapter which cannot be used in dealing with the averages as herein charted is the chapter dealing with targets. The reason for this is our abandonment of the constant volume on the "X" axis. When we
did this all columns no longer represented the same amount of volume. Therefore,
point counts cannot be made. In addition, gaps are of little value, since they almost
never occur in a chart of the averages. Even on the few times that they do occur
they seem to have very little predictive value.

CHAPTER XII

CHARTING COMMODITIES

Since Equivolume charting is effective in analyzing stock action it naturally occurs to the trader that it might be worthwhile to apply the same methods to the commodity markets. After all, it is in commodities that extremely short term trading can be used effectively. Margins amount to about ten percent of the value of the commitment, thereby magnifying moves by a factor of ten. Since the trader usually puts up about one dollar for each ten dollars worth of commodities he controls, a ten percent move in the price of the futures contract can either double his money or wipe him out. In addition, price moves are usually not long in coming, avoiding the impatience which we all occasionally experience when our stocks seem to be doing nothing. The trader who wants instant action can get it in commodities.

It would appear that Equivolume charting would be ideally suited to commodities trading, since the requirements of price and volume figures are met, and it appears to be a supply and demand market. There are some major differences between stocks and commodities, however. The first is the fact that there is not a fixed supply of contracts to offset demand. The number of contracts outstanding fluctuates widely, even during a given trading session.

If a person wants to buy 100 shares of General Motors he must buy it from someone who is willing to sell shares which he had previously bought. (This excludes the special case of buying a new issue of stock from an underwriter.) There are only a certain number of shares of General Motors outstanding, and new shares cannot be created to satisfy the desire of a buyer to own the stock.

On the other hand, if one person wishes to buy a contract of May Wheat and another person wishes to sell a contract of the same commodity, with the same delivery date, they can enter into a futures contract, thereby creating a new contract that did not exist prior to their transaction. Since demand was met by creation instead of delving into supply our supply-demand equilibrium is no longer valid. This is the first drawback to applying Equivolume methods to commodities.

The second drawback is closely related to this. Commodities contracts are not everlasting. They do not begin until a certain date, and they expire a number of months later. When a new delivery month starts trading there are no contracts outstanding, and both supply and demand are at zero. From this time onward contracts are created, and traded. The total contracts outstanding is called the open interest. The open interest begins at zero, reaches a peak sometime before delivery, and finally returns to zero on the last day of trading. Consequently trading volume in the contract follows the same pattern. If we were to chart a commodities contract, using the volume in that delivery month only we would have a very unreliable chart. It would reflect the increase and decrease in volume due to the swings in open interest, rather than the anomalies caused by buying and selling pressures. In order to somewhat eliminate the problem we chart total volume for all traded months, in the particular commodity, rather than the volume for the single delivery month whose price we are charting.

In using this method of expressing volume we have eliminated one problem and introduced a new problem. It is the same one we ran into in the chapter on charting the averages, the combining of figures, and ending up with days that are too uniform. In order for Equivolume charting to be helpful there must be a sensitivity to changes in volume. Adding together the volumes for all months traded tends to somewhat eliminate this sensitivity. In addition, the heaviest trading is usually in the trading month which is closest to delivery. If we are watching a different month, we may be overly influenced by volume which should not directly concern us.

The third difference between stocks and commodities involves trading limits. Commodities exchanges set limits to the amount which prices can move within a given trading session. When this limit is reached trading halts. Thereby the supply-demand equilibrium is disrupted. Prices are not being allowed to reach their normal level. Instead of heavy trading, which could be expected on a major move, we get no trading at all.

The reader will gather from the foregoing paragraphs that Equivolume charting is useless for commodities trading. This conclusion is not altogether correct. At times the charts will show up tops and bottoms very effectively, and moves through resistance areas are usually easily recognized. The trader in commodities will find, however, that he cannot depend on these charts as much as he could with stock charts.

Often the classic signals which we have come to rely upon in trading stocks will be absent from commodities charts even at major turning points. Trend lines are usually reliable, but on the other hand, gaps are very unreliable.

In short, let us say that Equivolume charts are helpful in commodities trading but do not provide an instant road to riches. The drawbacks which are caused by the difference between commodities markets and stock markets at least offset the advantage of small margin and no interest charges. (See Figures 35 and 36.)

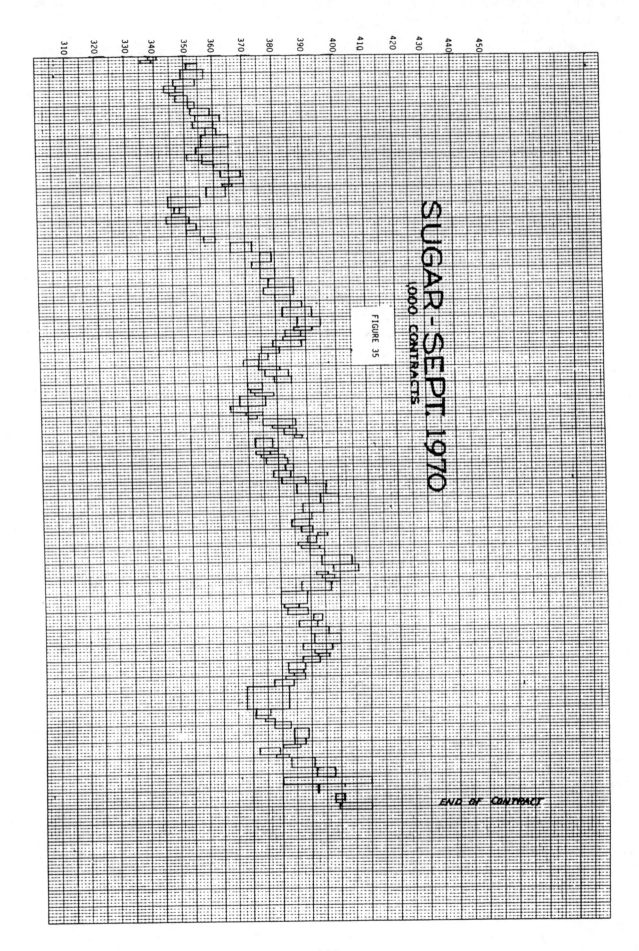

SUGAR-SEPT.1970

1000 CONTRACTS

FIGURE 35

END OF CONTRACT

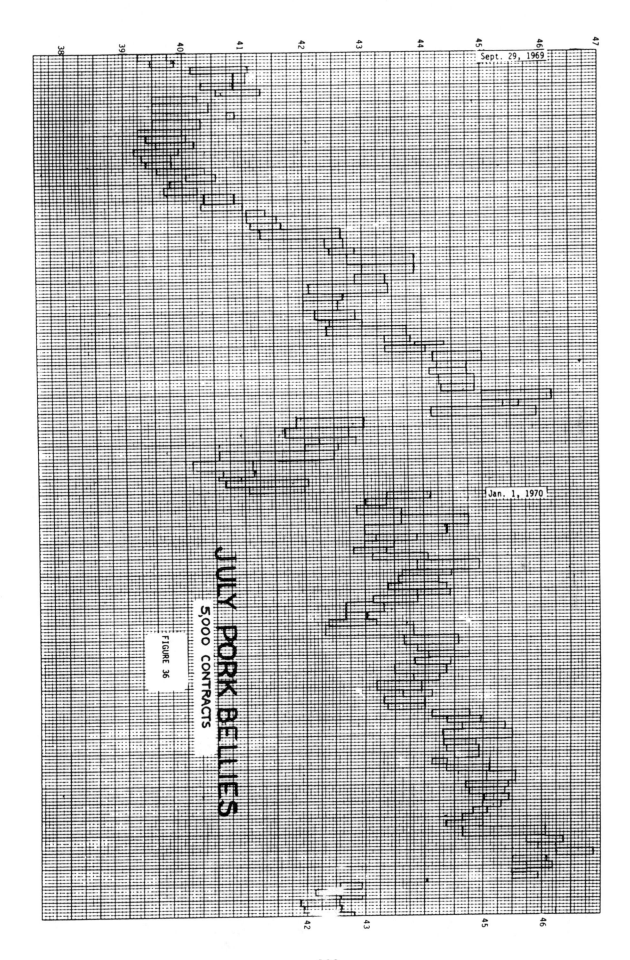

JULY PORK BELLIES
5,000 CONTRACTS

FIGURE 36

Sept. 29, 1969

Jan. 1, 1970

CHAPTER XIII

THE SHORT TERM TRADING INDEX

Every stock is both a good buy and a good short sale at given points in time. In fact, it is often amazingly easy, using the foregoing chapters, to recognize stocks which are good buys. However, each of us has gone through the distress of selecting what appears to be an excellent situation only to watch the market start to slide, and our stock drop with it. Yet nothing has changed within the company. The change has been in investor sentiment.

The problem is not selection, but timing. When the market is in an extended down move the stocks that go up in the face of it are few. To try to select those issues which are going to buck such a move is to fight high adverse odds. Sure, you may be able to find those stocks which are going to buck the trend, but it is far easier to make money if you recognize the direction of the market and go with it. There are times when the market is so strong that picking a bad stock is next to impossible, and other times when almost no stocks, regardless of basic value, are going to bring you a profit.

Timing of your actions in the market will allow you to be long at the right time, and then either out of the market or short during the down swings. in this chapter we will be working with an index which can help to provide this timing.

The Necessary Information. Although only a small amount of information is developed during a single trading session on a single stock (its price movement and its volume) when daily activity on an entire stock exchange is considered, the total information is huge. Most newspapers publish this information, but only recently has the electronic computer made it possible to quickly group and correlate this information.

Such is the case with the figures used for this index. With the advent in recent years of electronic quotation devices on every broker's desk, a set of new and very interesting figures has become available. These are 1) the number of stocks which are showing gains for the day; 2) the number of stocks which are showing losses for the day; 3) the total number of shares traded in those advancing issues; and 4) the total number of shares traded in the declining issues. These factors are constantly tabulated and updated by the computers which provide the information for the interrogation units. Simply by pushing a few buttons on the machine one can get these figures up-to-the-minute. In fact, at least one of these quotation systems has programmed the short term index into its computer, so that you need not even make the computations explained in the next section. The quotation machine carries the index fully computed and updated.

Calculation of the Short Term Trading Index. The calculation of this index is relatively simple and can be easily run through on a slide rule or a small desk calculator. The equation is as follows:

$$\dfrac{\dfrac{\text{ADVANCES}}{\text{DECLINES}}}{\dfrac{\text{ADVANCING VOLUME}}{\text{DECLINING VOLUME}}} = \text{Short Term Trading Index}$$

Let us suppose that at a given time 485 stocks are up and 612 are down. Then the numerator is the ratio of 485 to 612. At the same time let us suppose that the volume on the advancing issues is 2,780,000 shares and the volume on the declining issues is 3,650,000 shares. The denominator is 2,780,000 divided by 3,650,000.

The final calculation would be as follows:

$$\dfrac{\dfrac{485}{612}}{\dfrac{2,780,000}{3,650,000}} = \dfrac{.793}{.762} = 1.04$$

Most modern quotation devices carry these figures revised every few minutes, so the analyst is able to calculate the index as often as he wishes throughout the trading session.

To make the index more understandable, and especially the reasoning behind it, let us consider a simpler example. Suppose that the market has just opened and only two stocks have traded so far. One stock is up and the other is down. Looking at this alone it would appear to be a standoff sort of market. Whether one had moved more than the other in terms of points will probably mean very little also, since they are different companies with different volatilities and different price ranges. Let us also assume, however, that the up stock has traded 500 shares and the down stock has traded 1000 shares. This changes the picture. The volume on the up stock is only

half the volume on the down stock. This obviously indicates that the selling pressure

is more dominant than the buying pressure. The situation, in this overly simple ex-

ample, is bearish.

The equation for the index would appear as follows:

Advances = 1

Declines = 1

Advancing Volume = 500

Declining Volume = 1000

$$\frac{\dfrac{1}{1}}{\dfrac{500}{1000}} = \frac{1}{.5} = 2.00$$

Any index which is over 1.00 is bearish while any index under 1.00 is bullish. The

above example would be considered a very bearish index.

If, instead there had been 500 shares on the down stock and 1000 shares on

the up stock, the index would be .50 and would be construed as a bullish indication.

The buyers were more aggressive than the sellers.

Thus, the index is measuring the aggressiveness of the buyers and sellers. It

compares the ratio of buyers to sellers with the ratio of buying volume to selling

volume. Basically it asks the question "Are the 'up' stocks getting their share of the

volume?" If the index comes out to 1.00 it is a standoff market since the volume on up stocks is in the same proportion as the volume on down stocks. If the index is less than unity, however, then those stocks which are "up" are getting more than their share of the volume. Traders are evidently anxious to own stocks since those stocks which are generating the heaviest market volume are moving up. This must therefore be a bullish sign.

If the index is more than 1.00 then the greatest proportionate volume is occurring in these stocks which are showing losses. Evidently, then, the traders are more anxious to sell than to buy. They are doing most of their trading in stocks which are showing losses, so they are evidently willing to sell at price concessions, and are pushing prices down.

Very often this index will point out a market sentiment which is entirely opposite from that which could be construed from any other indicator. For example, more stocks can be up than down, giving a bullish advance-decline line, and at the same time the popular averages may be in plus territory, yet the bulk of the volume will be in the declining issues, giving a negative short term trading index. Only this new index is pointing out that the reins are in the hands of the sellers rather than the buyers. In this sort of situation the entire market will almost invariably turn lower before long.

What happens is simple. The market has been moving up and buyers have been coming into the market in increasing numbers. At some time, however, the people who are in for a relatively small move but who control vast amounts of capital reach a point where they are ready to cash in. They begin to sell into the general market strength. Because they are traders they are looking for maximum moves but necessarily must deal in stocks sufficiently active to provide a market which can absorb large block movement.

Traders must trade in the volatile and liquid stocks. Consequently they are in the Xeroxes, Polaroids, Sperry Rands, or whatever happens to fall into that category in that type market. Such stocks day after day are somewhere near the top of the most active list. As traders liquidate, they drive these stocks into minus territory and all of their volume is now attributed to the down side of the market. Meantime, the less active stocks that make up the bulk of the market, but not the bulk of the trading, still are registering gains and consequently keeping the averages up. But the selling has already begun and will soon spread to the other issues. The intent of the traders has shown itself but can only be spotted by this index.

Exactly the opposite type of action occurs in a down market. The traders start to acquire stocks near the bottom of the down move. They naturally move into the active issues, and soon push them into the column of advancing issues rather than declining issues. This generated volume is then attributed to the plus side of the market. This activity pushes the index below 1.00 demonstrating buying activity. This usually happens while most stocks are still down and any index, whether the Dow-Jones Industrials or the more widely based indices such as the Standard and Poors Composite, is still in minus territory. Only this indicator promptly shows what is actually happening.

In capitalizing on market turns it is extremely important to move fast. A few minutes can mean a few points in the type of stocks and the type of market moves we are discussing here. Consequently an index must be sensitive and unequivocal. Experience has shown that this Short Term Trading Index meets both these criteria.

The Index as a Timing Technique. It has been found that there are two important uses for the Short Term Trading Index. One is a timing technique, and the other is as a trading technique. We will deal first with the timing function, for it is here that it has a value for the largest number of market participants.

It would be well first to hark back to the often repeated analogy between the stock market and the ocean. The market is made up of long term phases which last many months or even years in which stock prices are in a general uptrend or a general downtrend. These long moves could be compared to the tides on the ocean. Superimposed on these moves are shorter term up and down swings in the market which compare to the waves in the ocean. Finally there are the very short term moves which last only a few hours or days, and, in the analogy are described as the ripples on the ocean.

The tidal moves of the stock market are based on long term economic considerations, and can be interpreted by studies of economic trends. Similarly, the waves are based primarily on hard, tangible facts but of lesser importance than the major factors which decide the tidal patterns. The ripples, however, are quite different. They are the result of the millions of emotional factors which trigger surges of buying or selling. They are the minute by minute result obtained from the balancing of the two dominant stock market emotions: Fear and Greed. Many analysts would argue that there are fundamental factors which bring about these emotions and cause the ripples. This is true, but their interpretation is almost impossible. In fact, most analysts ignore the ripples, and say, "If the stock is a buy, then buy it. The day to day minor fluctuations are small as related to the overall results expected, based on the fundamentals."

The day to day fluctuations are important. The difference between the top and the bottom of the trading range of a stock can easily be five or ten percent of the price of the stock. If you are interested in buying a stock priced in the low twenties and anticipate a move to the low thirties, it is very important whether you pay twenty-one or twenty-three for the stock. You were expecting a fifty percent profit, but you may be giving away twenty percent of that profit. If you are more conservative, and trying to make twenty percent on your average successful trade, it can cut that profit in half. The use of this index can help you to time purchases or sales so that this is less likely to happen. This index cannot take the place of good judgment in selecting stocks. It can, however, help you to decide whether to buy this morning or hold off until this afternoon or tomorrow.

In order to make use of the index, the stock trader or his broker should calculate the index quite often. In a fast moving market it may be necessary to check it every half hour. When things are quieter, or the market direction is fairly obvious, two or three times a day is sufficient. The idea is to spot changes in the index. The direction in which the index is moving, and the speed at which it is taking place are at least as important as the numerical value of the index. In addition, constant use of the index will develop a "feel" for it which cannot be developed in any other way.

Reproduced below, just as it originally appeared in Barron's is a table which shows how this index should be interpreted by the stock trader. Let me point out again, however, that the investor should not merely use this table, without trying to develop a "feel" for its use. He should either become proficient himself or deal with a broker who constantly uses and interprets the index.

Table A - Rising Market

1. Index bearish. (i.e., greater than 1.00).
    a) Improving (i.e., becoming lower). Upward move to continue.
    b) Deteriorating (i.e., becoming higher). Market will turn down, but not necessarily immediately. This condition can continue for some time, perhaps for as much as two days.
2. Index bullish (i.e., less than 1.00).
    a) Improving (i.e., becoming lower). Move to continue upward.
    b) Deteriorating (i.e., becoming higher). If it occurs slowly as market advances, it is normal. However, rapid deterioration is a strong bear signal.

Table B - Falling Market

1. Index bearish.
    a) Improving. As in 2-b above, normal improvement unless a rapid turn. Then a very bullish signal.
    b) Deteriorating. Decline to continue.

2. Index bullish.
    a) Improving. Market will turn up, but not necessarily immediately. It may take as much as two days of this condition before a turn.
    b) Deteriorating.
       Selling not yet completed, decline likely to continue.

The headings "Rising Market" and "Declining Market" refer only to the daily figures.

The most easily obtained and most often updated market measure is the Dow-Jones

Industrial Average. This average is perfectly satisfactory for our use.

The most important moves are those in which a sudden swing occurs. For example, let us suppose that the market has been down for the last few days, with the index holding in the 1.00 to 1.50 range. This morning prices were again lower and the index was even more bearish, at 1.70. Now, at mid-session the index has suddenly swung all the way across to a .75 although there has been little or no improvement in the popular averages. This is the time to buy! The rapid change in the index has tipped the hand of the traders. They are accumulating the active stocks and changing the entire market tempo. This move, and its counterpart when the index rapidly swings very bearish after a period of advancing prices, are the most reliable and usually most profitable signals the index gives.

As another example, let's suppose that you are convinced that stock prices over the intermediate or long term are going lower. In addition, you have picked out the stock which you feel is the best possible short sale. Today, however, the market opened slightly higher, and has continued to advance slowly. The index has remained in bullish territory, but has changed little during the day. It is now .83. It would be pointless to short your stock now. If it follows the market, you are likely to be able to short it at a higher level since there is no indication that the market is through going up. You will probably do better if you wait until the index starts to go bearish. Even then, if it is a slow move with the averages also giving ground you may want to hold off on the short, depending upon the action of the stock you are watching. If, however, the index swings rapidly, and especially if it precedes any weakening in the averages, you should establish your short position immediately.

We have assumed in the above section that your stock is going to follow the market. There is, of course, the danger that it will not. It is best, therefore, to work with stocks that have in the past followed market moves rather than countering them. In addition, low volume issues are less reliable than active stocks. They may be very slow in following market trends. There is plenty of money to be made in the well-known active issues without ever searching out the off-beat stocks that only trade a few hundred shares a day.

The Index as a Trading Technique. It was pointed out previously that the "ripples" in the market can be important in timing trades. These ripples can be even more important to the short term trader. He is not only trying to improve his position by capitalizing them but also he is trying to base his entire market strategy on the use of these ripples.

A person who is buying a stock or selling it short with the intention of only holding the position for a few days and taking a relatively small profit cannot be concerned with long term fundamental considerations. An excellent fundamental picture, such as skyrocketing earnings, may determine the long term direction of the stock, but is unlikely to have a predictable effect upon the price action over a few days. The short term trader must recognize the patterns of the market, and try to capitalize on the minor swings which provide him his profit potentials. Especially, he must be cognizant of the emotionalism of his marketplace. As selling begins to come into the market the trader must act quickly and join the selling as early as possible. Similarly, as buyers start to gain the upper hand he must be ready to es-

tablish long positions.

It has been found that this index provides the trader with an excellent tool.

His use of the index is somewhat different from that of the longer term investor and

must be treated separately. Basically, the trader should sell every time the index

turns decidedly bearish and buy every time the index turns decidedly bullish. In this

way he is always going with the market. Since the market cannot go down very long

without the index going bearish, the trader is never locked into a position which is

contrary to the general market trend. Conversely, if the market is going up, the in-

dex either is bullish or soon will be. Thus, the index provides the same advantage

as a stop order. The trader cannot stay wrong long.

Although 1.00 is the true standoff market, it has been found that a reading

on the index which falls between about .75 and 1.25 is "normal" and could be termed

the trading range of the index. Any index below .75 is decidedly bullish while any

reading over 1.25 is decidedly bearish. Usually as the market turns bullish it will go

well below .75 and then return to the normal area as the upward move progresses. At

the end of the upward move it will go decidedly bearish, usually before prices turn

back down. It will then stay within the trading range until the decline is over, at

which time another extreme index reading in the bullish direction will occur. In or-

der to use this index for short term trading the speculator should buy on every ex-

tremely bullish index reading and then close out his purchases and establish short

positions when the index goes above 1.25.

This certainly sounds simple, doesn't it? It isn't! It takes a great deal of work and practice to become proficient in analyzing the action of the index. Sometimes it will appear to be just about to give a buy signal, only to quickly turn bearish again. Other times it will give a buy signal and reverse itself in a few hours of trading. There is no way in which a trader can be successful on every commitment. If he wants to make money using this index he must stay close to it, and learn to understand the signals the index gives. In addition, he must be able to make rapid decisions. If the index says "buy now" he must act immediately. This sort of trading is dependent on every eighth of a point. To be right on a stock is not enough. It must move far enough to pay commissions and still show a profit. As was pointed out in the previous section, not only the numerical value of the index but also the speed of change in this value are important. When the index very rapidly goes to a bullish reading there is no question but that the trader should buy. If, however, after a sell signal is in effect the index drifts slowly to the bullish side, even exceeding the .75 criterion there is a question as to the legitimacy of the signal. We have found that this sort of action, occurring more slowly, calls for a slower response. The drift into bullish territory may turn prices upward, but the turn will also occur slowly. If prices do follow the index or it goes more bullish the trader must then correct his position, and stay with the market trend.

We all tend to ignore unpleasantness. This is especially true if we own a stock and it and the market start to go against us. If you are a speculator trying to capitalize on the ripples in the market, you must be able to admit that you were wrong, or that you were right about the market but wrong about the stock you used. The biggest pitfall in this kind of trading is to allow the market to convert your short-term speculation into a long-term investment. If you do you will find yourself with a long position in a declining market, and nothing to do but wait for the next up-cycle.

The mechanics of using this system are simple. Either stay close to the market yourself or make sure that your broker does. Calculate the index often. You should be able to spot an important shift in trader sentiment within a few minutes. If your broker is watching the market for you, you must be readily available. When he calls you must make an immediate decision. A few minutes can be costly. When you decide to buy or sell, place market orders. Putting a price limit on your order can result in your being locked into an unfavorable situation. The key to the system is split second timing, and this can only be accomplished by buying and selling at the going price at that point in time.

For this sort of trading in any market transaction stock selection is extremely important. Here the criteria are different, however. Rather than earnings trends and dividend returns, you must look at price and volatility. Since you are interested in fairly small price moves it is better to deal in higher priced stocks. The commission rate is lower in proportion to the price moves, making the commission easier to regain. The limiting factor on this, however, is dependent upon your resources, since you should be dealing in multiples of 100 shares. Trades of less than 100 shares (Odd Lots) are dependent upon a prior 100 share trade, which may be damaging to your timing, since you do not necessarily get an immediate execution of your order. In addition, odd lots are transacted with a small price penalty. This can cut into your potential profit. Buy the higher priced stocks so that commissions are not eating up your profits, and stick to 100 share lots.

The stocks you use should be volatile, but should follow the market. Ideally, you should deal in stocks that usually go up when the market goes up, and down when the market goes down, but should move further than the market, proportionately.

Usually it is better not to use the same stocks for both long and short positions. Try to pick one set of stocks for the up-cycles and another set of stocks for the down-cycles. In addition, the stocks you use should be fairly heavy traders. They do not have to head the most active list, but they must have enough trading to allow you to move in and out of them rapidly, and without greatly changing the price through your own market activity.

Usually after you establish a position you will stay with it about three days. Sometimes a cycle will be very short, and other times very long. It would be unusual, however, to hold a position for more than ten days. Sometimes, of course, the phase will be so short that you will not even cover commissions, but you must act immediately, and stay with the market trend. The next move may be a long and very profitable one. Above all, you must not ignore a signal and consequently be long when you should be short, or vice versa. It can be an interesting and rewarding method of trading but it leaves no room for wishful thinking.

CHAPTER XIV

LONG TERM APPLICATIONS OF THE INDEX

When the index described in the preceding chapter first was made public it was called The Short Term Trading Index. The reason for this was its obvious applicability to the very short term market swings. Since the index first was published in Barrons, however, many people, including this author, have attempted to find ways in which it could be used as a longer term indicator.

It is logical that this type of application should work well. The index is directly measuring how anxious the public is to buy or sell. If, over a period of time the majority of volume is in the advancing issues, then there is obviously an upward pressure on the market. Conversely, a prolonged bias to the sell side is going to eventually force prices lower. It is necessary, however, to find methods which show us what is likely to happen in the future, rather than just a record of what has already happened.

The most obvious way of working with this sort of index is some sort of a moving average. The logical starting point, and the most widely used at this time, is a ten-day moving average. Figures 37 and 38 show the Standard and Poor 500 stock index at the top, and below this the ten-day moving average of the index, that is, it

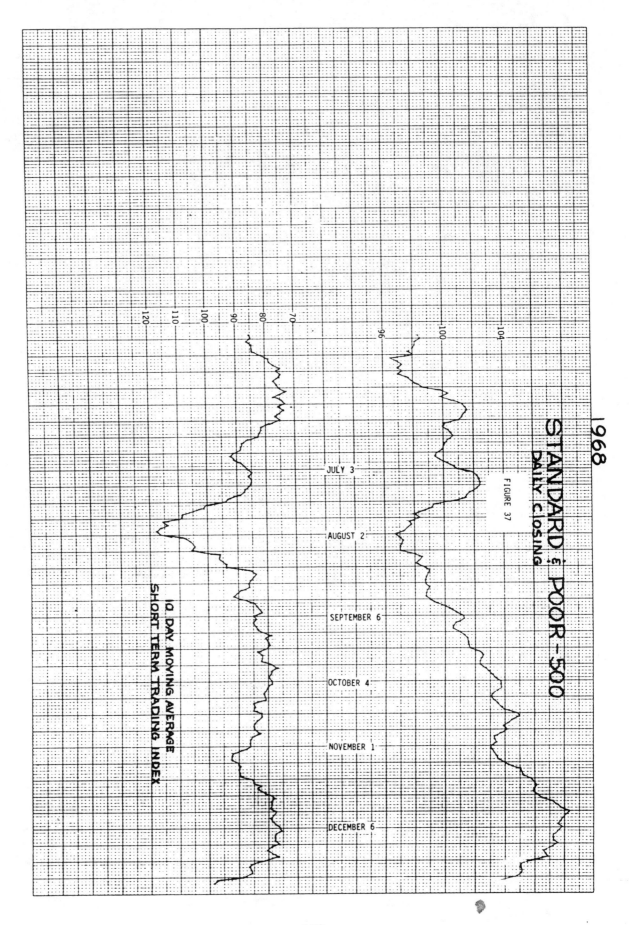

STANDARD & POOR-500
DAILY CLOSING

1968

FIGURE 37

JULY 3

AUGUST 2

SEPTEMBER 6

OCTOBER 4

NOVEMBER 1

DECEMBER 6

10 DAY MOVING AVERAGE
SHORT TERM TRADING INDEX

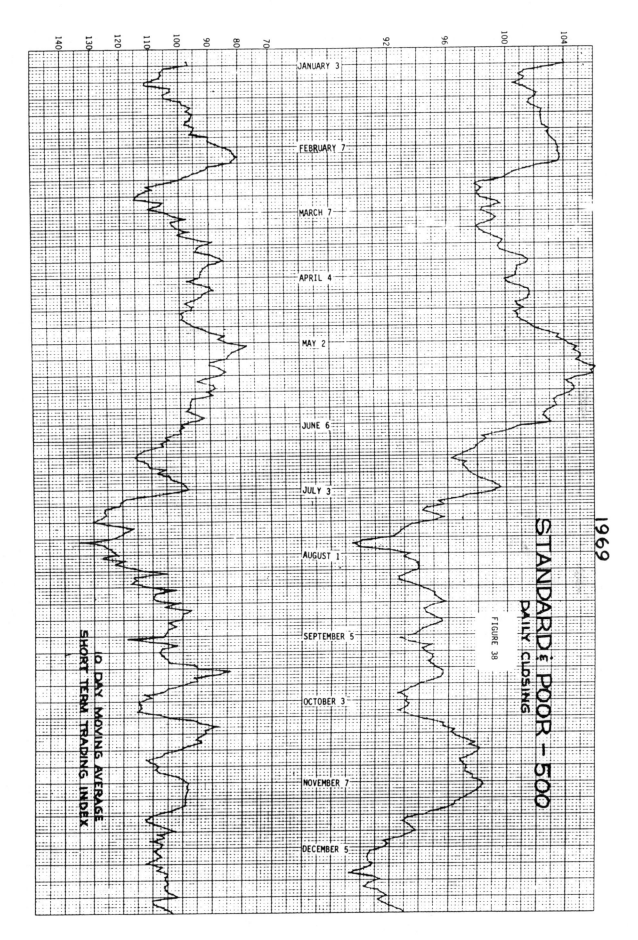

1969

STANDARD & POOR - 500
DAILY CLOSING

FIGURE 38

10 DAY MOVING AVERAGE
SHORT TERM TRADING INDEX

hits its tops and bottoms at the same time as the market does. Where the market may embark upon long advances or declines, the index tends to fluctuate about an area, going to high readings on market bottoms and low readings at market tops. Its function, then, is as an "overbought" and "oversold" indicator. Looking at not only the included charts, but at records that go back to 1965, when the advance decline volume figures first became available, it is possible to arrive at some quite reliable rules for trading using the ten-day moving average of the index.

We must first go back to the idea that the market behaves much like the ocean, with major market moves, corresponding to the tides, intermediate moves superimposed upon these tidal moves, which we will call the waves, and finally ripples superimposed upon the waves. The investor can try to take advantage of only the major market moves, or he can try to capitalize on the waves or the ripples. As he moves to the shorter term trading he increases his risk but also increases the possible rewards. The index can be used as an indicator for all three types of market trading, with its accuracy of course greater for the long term than for the short term.

The following brackets can be used:

SHORT TERM

When index is less than 75	SELL
When index is more than 105	BUY

INTERMEDIATE TERM

When index is less than 70	SELL
When index is more than 110	BUY

LONG TERM

When index is less than 60	SELL
When index is more than 150	BUY

All of the above values of course refer to the ten-day moving average of the index.

It should again be pointed out that this system is reliable but not foolproof. In an extremely bearish market the intermediate and short term tops may fail to reach the levels where they will give a sell signal as outlined in the preceding table. An astute trader should still be able to exercise some judgment, and recognize the end of the advance. Similarly, in a very strong bull market there may be only shallow dips which indicate the bottom of the short term decline has been reached. There is still no substitute for good judgment.

The accompanying table shows what sort of results would have been realized using these signals from June 1966 to November 1967. We show only the values of the Standard and Poor 500 on each of the trade days. With proper stock selection it is conceivable that the results could be even better. The table is hypothetical in the sense that it assumes an equal dollar investment in each of the securities composing the Standard and Poor 500.

In addition to the foregoing information in which a ten-day moving average was used, many other applications have been tried, and discarded. These include moving averages which are longer and shorter term. It appears that longer term moving averages only increase the delay between a turn and a signal, while the very short term moving averages make the pattern so wild as to be almost impossible to interpret. Point and figure charts of the index, or of moving averages of the index

have also been largely a waste of time, although one institutional investor has re-

ported good results using this sort of application to recognize the very long term mar-

ket swings. It still appears that the most obvious, the ten-day moving average is the

best to use.

TABLE 1

A   SHORT TERM

		BUY	S P	SELL	S P 500
1.	Long	June 7, 1966	84.80	June 21, 1966	86.70
2.	Short	July 29, 1966	83.60	June 21, 1966	86.70
*3.	Long	July 29, 1966	83.60	Aug. 15, 1966	83.15
4.	Short	Aug. 26, 1966	76.50	Aug. 15, 1966	83.15
5.	Long	Aug. 26, 1966	76.50	Dec. 12, 1966	83.00
6.	Short	Jan. 3, 1967	80.30	Dec. 12, 1966	83.00
7.	Long	Jan. 3, 1967	80.30	March 2, 1967	87.70
*8.	Short	April 3, 1967	89.20	March 2, 1967	87.70
9.	Long	April 3, 1967	89.20	May 23, 1967	91.75
10.	Short	June 9, 1967	91.50	May 23, 1967	91.75
11.	Long	June 9, 1967	91.50	June 19, 1967	92.50
12.	Short	Nov. 13, 1967	92.00	June 19, 1967	92.50
13.	Long	Nov. 13, 1967	92.00	April 6, 1968	93.75

Total Gains	34.50
Total Losses	1.95
Overall Gain	32.55
Long Only Gain	20.65
Short Only Gain	11.90

LONG TERM APPLICATIONS

B   INTERMEDIATE

		BUY			SELL	
1.	Long	Aug. 1, 1966	82.25	Aug. 15, 1966		83.15
2.	Short	Aug. 26, 1966	75.90	Aug. 15, 1966		83.15
3.	Long	Aug. 26, 1966	75.90	March 16, 1967		90.25
4.	Short	Nov. 14, 1967	91.40	March 16, 1967		90.25

Total Gains   22.50
Total Losses   1.15

Overall Gain   21.35

Long Only Gain   +15.25
Short Only Gain   + 6.10

C   LONG TERM

LONG TERM   SELL   Sept. 27, 1965   S&P at   90.75
LONG TERM   BUY   Sept. 6, 1966   S&P at   76.95

About the Author:

RICHARD W. ARMS, Jr, is a financial consultant to institutional investors and a private portfolio manager based in Albuquerque, New Mexico. He is a noted expert in the field of technical and market analysis, 1995 winner of the prestigious Market Technicians Award, and the author of several best selling books and articles on his groundbreaking theories in volume analysis and market theory. With over 30 years of experience as a financial analyst and advisor, Mr. Arms is perhaps best known for the development of one of the most reliable methods of long-term market forecasting: The Arms Index. This key technical tool for understanding market price movement is listed daily in the *Wall Street Journal* and is flashed once a minute on CNBC. Other market books by Mr. Arms include: *The Arms Index, Trading Without Fear,* and *Volume Cycles in the Stock Market.*

Barron's calls him...

"The technician's technician."

His theories have revolutionized the way investors perceive the market. And now, Dick Arms' groundbreaking work in technical analysis and charting is back in print, ready for a new generation of traders to learn - and profit - from.

PROFITS IN VOLUME is the original work on the "Equivolume" charting method developed by renowned market technician Richard Arms, Jr. In fact, his impact on the market is so significant that the Equivolume charting system is now part of most stock and futures software programs, including the popular MetaStock program.

Plus ...

- His Arms Index, also known as the Short-Term Trading Index (TRIN) - is so important to understanding the markets that it's featured daily in the *Wall Street Journal*.

- CNBC displays it across the ticker tape once every minute.

- His innovate work in Equivolume, volume weighted moving averages, ease of movement and other technical indicators earned him the prestigious Market Technicians Award in 1995.

- And his weekly fax service provides key research that top institutional investors and portfolio managers rely on.

Now, PROFITS IN VOLUME reacquaints investors with the basic concepts that form the foundation of his long-proven theories, and presents a reliable method of long-term market forecasting. Clear, uncomplicated language makes the book accessible to all investors - and a valuable addition to any investment library.